THE ... AND
THE PRIESTHOOD

DECLARATION

We humbly lay each and every one of the following pages at the feet of the infallible Vicar of Jesus Christ, and we submit in advance to the judgement of the Holy Church and of the Sovereign Pontiff, to whom we offer our most filial, most respectful and most entire obedience.

Dedicated by the Translator and his Brother to the memory of their dear Parents.

THE SACRED HEART
AND
THE PRIESTHOOD

By
Mother Louise Margaret Claret de la Touche

Translated from the French by
Rev. Patrick O'Connell, B.D.

TAN Books
An Imprint of Saint Benedict Press, LLC
Charlotte, North Carolina

IMPRIMI POTEST: ✠ JACOBUS
                  EPISCOPUS FERNENSIS

NIHIL OBSTAT: JACOBUS BROWNE
                  CENSOR DEPUTATUS

        DIE 19A JUNII 1950

Originally published by Fr. Patrick O'Connell and the Irish members of "The Priests' Universal Union of the Friends of the Sacred Heart."

Library of Congress Catalog Card Number: 79-90487

ISBN: 978-089555-128-3

Cover design by Tony Pro.

Printed and bound in the United States of America.

TAN Books
An Imprint of Saint Benedict Press, LLC
Charlotte, North Carolina
2012

Foreword to the First Edition

The Sacred Heart and the Priesthood was first written in French and published in Italy in 1910 during the reign of Pope Pius X. An Italian translation followed soon after. Subsequently it was translated into German, Polish, Dutch, Spanish, Croatian, Roumanian and Chinese. The present English translation was made in China at the same time as the Chinese translation, for the use of English-speaking priests in China and the Far East. This translation has been carefully revised and compared with the Italian version which was made during the lifetime of the author, and in case of doubt about the meaning, the Italian interpretation has been followed.

Mother Louise Margaret regarded herself as bound to convey the message of love contained in these books as simply as possible without any attempt at style. All translators are requested by those who hold the copyright to follow the original closely.

The first French edition was published anonymously for reasons explained below, but the intention of the author was that the origin of the book and all information that would help to make the message contained in it understood and appreciated should be furnished later on. This the translator has endeavored to do in the account of the author and her Mission which follows. For the full understanding, however, of both *The Sacred Heart and the Priesthood* and *The Book of Infinite Love,* the three volumes of the Intimate Notes published in French under the title *In the Service of Jesus Priest,* should be read. The translator has already prepared a translation of these three volumes and proposes to publish it as soon as circumstances will permit. He is indebted to many friends in China and in Ireland for kind assistance and valuable suggestions; to these he tends his sincerest thanks.

PATRICK O'CONNELL

1st September, 1947.

His Holiness Pius X sent a letter of introduction through His Cardinal Secretary for State, Merry del Val. *The Book of Infinite Love* was published in 1928 in the reign of Pius XI who also gave a letter of introduction through his Cardinal Secretary Gasparri. His present Holiness, Pius XII imparted a special blessing to the translator for the publication of these books. An Irish translation will appear as soon as possible.

Foreword to the Second Edition

The First English translation of *The Sacred Heart and the Priesthood* has found its way to all parts of Ireland, England, Scotland, America, Australia and to far-off India and Africa, and the edition of 5,000 copies is already exhausted. Orders to hand for a further 5,000 copies have made this new edition necessary.

The first English edition was presented to His Holiness, Pope Pius XII and received a gracious letter of approbation, which we give on p. XXV.

This new edition is printed unchanged, except for the addition of a paragraph making clear a few points about the relations between the Priests' Universal Union of the Friends of the Sacred Heart and other clerical Unions namely: that the Priests' Universal Union is a separate organization with a special object of its own; that other clerical Unions that become affiliated with it do not come under its jurisdiction but only contract a spiritual bond; that members of affiliated Unions do not become thereby members of the Priests' Universal Union, but must join in the ordinary way if they wish to become so.

There was unavoidable delay in bringing out the edition in the Irish language which we promised, but we expect that it will be ready by the end of this year.

PATRICK O'CONNELL
9th June, 1950.

Table of Contents

Life of Mother Louise Margaret Claret de la Touche

Her Mission and Her Writings

" 'GOD IS LOVE.' (*John* 4:8). His great occupation is to love. He loves from eternity to eternity."

"God loves, but He wishes to be loved; Love has need of a return, and if the very bosom of the Divinity, the Father, and the Word and the Holy Ghost give such a perfect return that They love each other with the same love which is Their essence and Their being, in like manner God wishes to find outside Himself a reciprocity, relative indeed and proportioned to the created being, but nevertheless real. The creature has received everything from God and is bound to return everything to God; it is what it is only by God; it should employ its whole being for God." (From *Book of Infinite Love* by Mother Louise Margaret).

This is the very essence of the devotion to the Sacred Heart and indeed of all religion: to believe that God is Love, to believe that He loves all men, and to love Him in return with our whole heart—which of course includes that we love our fellowmen for the love of Him.

God is Love and He is immutable; He always acts by Love, the history of His dealings with man can be summed up in one word—'Love.' On the other hand, the history of man is one long story of ingratitude, of refusal to love, often even of hatred of everything good. Yet even when man's wickedness went to the extreme, God, Who is love, overwhelmed it with love. When our first parents, created by God, endowed with a superabundance of His favors, and even made participators in His own divine nature, rejected God and the whole supernatural order, God's reply was the Incarnation. The message of the Word Incarnate was a message of love; His life was a life of love; and having enunciated and explained by word and example the great mystery of the Love of God, He displayed His mangled body, nailed to the Cross, with His Sacred Heart pierced by a lance, as the final proof of the greatness of God's love for men and His divine claim to· be loved in return.

Could man ever again doubt of God's love or refuse to return it? Alas, in the course of centuries man's love for God grew cold, the crucifix lost its significance for him, he scarcely believed even that God loved him, not to speak of striving to love God in return. The reply of Our Saviour was to make a new revelation of love through St. Margaret Mary Alacoque. Our divine Saviour made this new revelation of love, not by words alone, but by displaying His Sacred Heart surmounted by a cross, surrounded with a crown of thorns, still showing the wound which was made by the lance, and burning with love for man like a mighty furnace that would consume the world, thus giving a living epitome of His life of love for man, and renewing His divine claim to be loved in return.

Although this devotion of love, the devotion to the Sacred Heart, has been propagated in every part of the world, not only is His loving appeal ignored by the multitude, but new depths of ingratitude and iniquity have been sounded, and the world in our time is turning completely from God. Once again it is by love that Jesus wishes to conquer. He selects another member of the order of the Visitation, Mother Louise Margaret, to be the bearer of His message of love to the priests of the world and through them to the faithful.

The message of love given to St. Margaret Mary was for all men and for all time. The content of this message has been most minutely examined by the Church, and the devotion to the Sacred Heart has received its fullest approval. Those who have practiced it have been visibly blessed by God, and Our Blessed Saviour has expressed through His new apostle how much His Sacred Heart has been consoled by the zeal of those who propagate it. Nevertheless, it remains true that new efforts are required on the part of His faithful servants to offset the tremendous activity of the powers of Hell in these last ages. It is still through devotion to His Sacred Heart that He wishes to renew the world; but He wishes His priests to study the devotion more deeply and to propagate it with greater ardor; and to help them in this work, He puts at their disposal all the treasures of His Sacred Heart. Through the bearer of His new message He says:

"I wish to conquer hatred by love. I will send my priests to diffuse love over the earth. I have given them My Heart in order that they may see the treasures of love that are in God, that, having drawn for themselves, they may draw for the world. Tell them to go and dispense everywhere the treasure of love."

"There are in this Sacred Heart parts still unexplored which He has kept for His priests; it is a domain which He has reserved for them. There are dwellings of love into which priests will enter, and where they will find all that they have need of to be faithful representatives of Jesus."

"The devotion to the Sacred Heart should not be, as too often happens, a vague, superficial, sentimental devotion, attached to the exterior object. Although very justly we may and ought to adore this Heart of flesh which is the real tabernacle of divine Charity, and most truly the Heart of God in virtue of the Hypostatic union, we should not, however, stop there but should penetrate by the opening of the Heart into the most profound mysteries of Infinite Love.

We should apply ourselves to this by a careful study of the holy Gospels, of the immortal Epistles of St. John and St. Paul, by the reading of the early Fathers and of the Catholic authors who have treated this admirable subject. We will thus acquire a true and solid devotion to the divine Heart and will be in a position to communicate it to the faithful who do not all yet understand the treasures of grace and regeneration which are there found."

Life of Mother Louise Margaret

Margaret Claret de la Touche, the author of *The Sacred Heart and the Priesthood* and of *The Book of Infinite Love,* was born at Saint Germain de Laye in France on March 15th, 1868. Her father died when she was seven years old. Her mother married again; her second husband being Mr. De Chamberet. In her childhood she met with an accident which affected her health for life. She writes: "The cross stood over my cradle: suffering was to be my lot, and to be the first sign of love given by Jesus to my soul."

The family in which she was brought up was a practicing Catholic family but could hardly be called pious. She describes religious life in her home as follows: "I have never seen a member of the family miss Mass on Sunday or the abstinence on Friday, except in case of real illness; all approached the Sacraments four times a year, seriously, to fulfill a duty. My mother got the Holy Sacrifice offered frequently for my father and for our deceased relatives; she gave large alms and urged us to practice charity; but for us God was only a just Master whom we must serve strictly, respect for His greatness, and leave alone in the heights of Heaven in the midst of His Angels and Saints."

She did not receive her first Communion till she was about eleven years old—"a Communion," she writes, "made in the innocence of childhood but without love." Her mother aimed at developing in her a strong Spartan character on the old pagan models; but not a word was said about the early Christian martyrs.

She had a fine library at her disposal from which she read deeply. She had an innate aversion to books attacking the Church or its teaching. She was forbidden to read the *Life of St. Therese* or any book likely to turn her mind to the religious life.

In spite of her gay and worldly environment she made a vow of virginity after her first Communion with a promise to enter a convent, if God favored her with a religious vocation.

In the gay life in which she was obliged to take part she made herself respected by all for her reserve and modesty. Once in a moment of weakness she thought of yielding to the wishes of her mother and marrying a young officer for whom she had formed an affection. She was thinking of getting dispensed from her vow when the temptation was providentially removed.

She renewed her vow of virginity and wept over this passing weakness till the end of her life.

On the advice of her confessor, she decided to enter a convent of the Visitation, at Romans, in the south of France—the same Order to which St. Margaret Mary belonged.

Obstacles that to a person of lesser virtue would have seemed insurmountable were placed in her way, but her determination could not be shaken. As a preparation for her entry into religious life, she made a pilgrimage to Paray-le-Monial during which she consecrated herself entirely to the Sacred Heart. Soon after, on November 20th, 1890, she entered the convent of the Visitation at Romans in France. She became an exemplary Sister, without allowing anything to appear that would draw attention to herself. Her natural defects brought her many humiliations and caused her much suffering, while her great talents and heroic sanctity were known of only by those whom God had given her to guide her. She received the white veil on October 17th, 1891, and was professed on the same date of the following year, being given the name in religion of Sister Louise Margaret.

Early in her religious life, she began to enjoy special favors from Our Divine Lord—favors like those of St. Margaret Mary. Her heroic fidelity to great graces received, and her willing acceptance of a life of suffering and contradictions, assured for her the continuation of those favors till the end of her life. As in the case of St. Margaret Mary, Our Lord sent her continuous bad health, frequent illnesses, humiliations, and contradictions to make her conformable to His own suffering life, and to fit her for the work for which He had destined her.

After her profession she enjoyed the constant presence of her divine Spouse in a manner similar to that in which St. Margaret Mary was favored. Like St. Margaret Mary, Our Lord allowed her also to share in a mysterious way in His own divine sufferings. Of this she writes as follows: "At prayer I suffered strangely. Our Saviour showed me a chalice which I must drink, so bitter that my human nature revolted against it with all its strength. I was as if in agony, but after a struggle, I accepted all; I consented to all and I abandoned myself to all." September, 1896: "Our Lord wishes that I be a victim immolated to His good pleasure and all consumed by the fire of His divine love. . . . My heart must be as an ardent flame burning my whole body without consuming it . . . . My divine Saviour gave me to understand that He chooses souls to continue His Passion in them, but as a human soul could not alone endure all His sufferings, He gives to each one a little part. He wishes to make me share in His state of painful crucifixion. His feet and hands were made fast: He was suspended without movement, suffering a slow and silent agony, no longer acting. He wishes that I remain thus under His action in the disposition to endure everything. . . . On the following morning, I awoke at 3 a.m. suffering inexpressible pains, and for more than an hour Our Saviour made me again share in His sufferings; I suffered acute pain in all my members, especially in my feet."

Her Mission

The ecclesiastical authorities have made no pronouncement as to whether or not she was favored with revelations from Our Lord ordering her to have a world-wide association of priests formed to promote devotion to the Sacred Heart, but they have given their "imprimatur" to books which publish these communications, subject to any decision that the Church may at any time make; furthermore, they have covered her message with the authority of the Church, and have sanctioned the association of priests to promote devotion to the Sacred Heart which, she states, Our Lord ordered her to get founded; and have adopted the statutes of the association which she, under obedience, drew up in conformity with what she believed to be Our Lord's wishes.

As has been already mentioned, Mother Louise Margaret felt, even from the time of her profession, that God had special designs on her soul. The nature of these designs was indicated to her, in a general way, in lights which she received in prayer during 1901.

It was on the Feast of the Sacred Heart 1902 and during the seven following days, now the Octave, that she received what she believed to be definite commands and definite instructions from Our Lord concerning her mission. These He ordered her to write down. The following is her account, written under obedience, of what took place during that Octave:

"Yesterday, on June 6th 1902, the Feast of the Sacred Heart, I was alone before the Most Blessed Sacrament. I was in that weary and painful state of mind in which I had been for some weeks, when Jesus made His presence felt. I adored Him, being sweetly consoled by His presence, and praying to Him for our little novitiate, I asked Him to give me some souls I might form for Him. He replied: 'I will give you souls of men.' Being profoundly astonished by these words, the sense of which I did not understand, I remained silent, endeavoring to find an explanation, till Jesus said: 'I will give you souls of priests.' Still more astonished I asked Him: 'My Jesus how wilt Thou do that?' He replied 'It is for My priests that you will immolate yourself; I wish to instruct you during this Octave. Write down all that I shall tell you.' "

"I did not wish to write any more, but I obeyed Jesus. Yesterday evening He said to me: 'My priest is My other self, I love him, but he must be holy. Nineteen centuries ago, twelve men changed the world, they were not men merely, but they were priests. Now, once more, twelve men could change the world.'

"On June 7th He said: 'Margaret Mary has shown My heart to the world, do you show it to My priests and draw them all to My Heart.'

"On June 8th, He showed me the greatness of the priest. Chosen from among men he reaches even up to God; he is placed between man and God, a mediator like Jesus, and with Jesus. He has been, so to speak, transubstantiated into Jesus, and he enters thus into His divine offices and His divine prerogatives. With Jesus he is sacrifice, expiation, victim. From this state of special union with Jesus all the acts of the priest acquire an incomprehensible excellence."

On June 10th she wrote: "After Communion I said to Jesus, 'My Saviour, when our Blessed Sister (Margaret Mary) showed Thy divine Heart to the world, did not Thy priests see It? Does not that suffice?' Jesus replied: 'I wish now to make a special manifestation to them.' Then He showed me that He has a special work to do, which is to enkindle the fire of love again in the world, and that He wished to make use of His priests to accomplish it. He said this with such a touching and tender expression that tears came to my eyes. 'I have need of them,' He said, 'to do My work, to extend the reign of love; they must be full of it themselves and it is to My Heart that they must come to draw it.' And He added: 'If anyone has the right, the duty, to drink out of My Heart, is it not My priests who each day bring the chalice of the altar to their lips? Let them come to My Heart and let them drink there.' "

Next day she wrote again: "All day yesterday I saw, as it were, a special group of priests around the Heart of Jesus: an organization exclusively for priests; I do not know whether I am deceived. When by myself I wish to think on what He communicates to me, I cannot do so, nothing clear or precise comes to my mind; on the contrary, as soon as He speaks or touches my soul with His divine impressions, everything is clear, luminous and definite.' "

Again, on the following day she writes: "This morning I thought that a special branch of the 'Guard of Honor' might be formed for priests. Jesus said: 'No. I do not wish that priests be merely adorers of My Heart. I wish to form an army of priests who will fight for the triumph of My Love. Those who will form part of this army will undertake, among other things, to preach Infinite Love and mercy, and to be united among themselves, having but one heart and one soul, and never impeding one another in their activities.' "

On June 25th she wrote: "I saw the priest as the most perfect image of the Word Incarnate. I saw the loving delight which the Three Persons of the most Blessed Trinity take in him. I saw the ineffable complacency of the Father contemplating in him the traits of His Son. I saw the complacency of the Son recognizing Himself in him. I saw the complacency of the Holy Ghost considering in him one of His finest masterpieces. Then I saw the return of love and service which the Most Blessed Trinity expects.

"The priest should not love God merely in a general way, as do the faithful; he should have a special sentiment of love for each of the Three Persons; for the Father, a love of adoration and filial respect, similar to the love of Jesus for His Father; for the Son, a love of union which keeps him in continuous relation with Him; for the Holy Ghost, a love of dependence, of docility and of recourse."[1]

The Publication of The Sacred Heart and the Priesthood

Mother Louise Margaret committed to writing the lights which she received and the commands given to her, and submitted them to her religious superior and to her director, Father Charrier, S.J. This Father Charrier was designated to her by Our Lord as the person who was to help her to carry out her mission. In his humility, he thought himself unworthy to take part in such a great work. For thirteen years he received from her a written account of all the lights and graces with which she had been favored. For seven years he had in his possession all the material for the book on *The Sacred Heart and the Priesthood* which

---

1. As time went on, the details of the divine plan were communicated to her. In 1910, she herself summarized this plan as follows: "A worldwide Priests' Union of the Friends of the Sacred Heart was to be formed. The object of this Union was: 1) to group the priests of the world around the adorable Heart of Our Lord Jesus Christ in order to array them as an elite body against the errors and corruption of our time; 2) to procure the personal sanctification of its members by a true and practical devotion to the Sacred Heart of Jesus, the Tabernacle of Infinite Love; and the sanctification of the faithful through the development and good direction of the apostolic zeal of the clergy; 3) to restore and develop the family spirit of solidarity in the sacerdotal body . . . and draw them in a close and filial union around their bishop." (From *The Book of Infinite Love*).

she had sent to him, requesting him to put it in order and have it published without allowing her name to appear.

Father Charrier hesitated, not because he doubted the fact that Mother Louise Margaret, as she asserted, had received communications from Our Divine Lord, but because he himself had been named as the person that was to aid in carrying out this great work. The hesitation of Father Charrier caused her much suffering, for she felt herself urged by Our Lord to have His message conveyed to His priests. In January, 1908, she wrote to him: "A few days ago at prayer, Our Lord communicated to me the immense desire which He has to be loved by His priests whom He Himself loves as His dearest members. *He wishes that they should all know that He has given them His Heart,* and it seems to me that He demands that you should write, or get someone to write, a little book which would contain all the desires He has for His priests and all His effusions of tender love for them, with a view to the foundation of this organization which is intended to group them around His Sacred Heart and in His Infinite Love."

On receipt of this letter, Father Charrier sent all the writings of Mother Louise Margaret to Father Hamon, S.J., an author who was well-known for his writings on devotion to the Sacred Heart. Father Hamon's reply was that "a little book should be composed from the writings of Mother Louise Margaret which would spread abroad the ideas contained in them." Father Charrier commenced the book in February, 1908, but he was kept so occupied with his priestly duties that at the end of a year he had written only the first eight pages of the proposed book.

In April, 1909, Mother Louise Margaret again wrote to him as follows: "It seems to me that Our Lord is not pleased with me. It is seven years since He said to me: 'Show My Heart to My priests': seven years since, on the Feast of the Sacred Heart and during the seven following days, He communicated to me what He desired from His priests, and told me of the treasures of love which He has in His divine Heart for them. . . It seems to me that Jesus is saying to me interiorly: 'I have entrusted you with a treasure, the treasure of My Infinite Love, and you have buried it in the ground.' "

Father Charrier finding that want of time made it impossible for him to compose the book, finally renounced the idea, and sent all the writings back to Mother Louise Margaret. She sent them to Father Poletti, the superior of the Priest-Adorers of the Blessed Sacrament, asking him to compose the book. He replied to her saying that "the book could not be the work of any other hand or heart but of the person who had received these communications from her divine Spouse." Father Choupin, S.J., was also consulted and he gave the same decision. Finally her bishop, Monsignor Filipello, having been informed of the whole matter, put Mother Louise Margaret under obedience to compose the book.

She obeyed. With infinite care she classified her notes and recast them into the beautiful form in which we find them in *The Sacred Heart and the Priesthood*. She herself was fully persuaded that there was not a single idea of her own in the book, but that all was from her divine Master. She always referred to it as "His Book." When it was published, she wrote to Father Charrier (April 9th, 1910): "Truly the divine Master Himself takes care of the interests of the little book. And it is right and just: *He is the Author of it.*" During her retreat of 1912, we find in her notes: "I have got the little book which Thou hast dictated to me published, I have poured into the heart of my bishop all that Thou hast given to me for Thy priests. What more can I do except pray and suffer?" When, after hesitating for seven years, Father Charrier, S.J., sent the manuscripts of Mother Louise Margaret to Father Poletti, he wrote: "It is indeed true that I do not pass judgment on the divine origin of the communications received by Mother Louise Margaret. But the sole reason is because I have not the right to do so; only the authority of the Church can pronounce on so delicate a matter. It nonetheless remains true that, as a private individual, I believe in this origin, because I have always found in the manner in which these communications have taken place, and in the nature of the communications themselves, such marks as, after long hesitation, have enabled me to reassure the Sister and sustain her." As we shall see later on, all the writings of Mother Louise Margaret were submitted to the Congregation of the Council and she herself was examined personally, with the result that her whole scheme— The Priest's Universal Union and the new convent of Sisters to serve as spiritual foundation for it—were approved of by this Congregation and received the support and blessing of His Holiness, Pope Pius X.

Nevertheless, it was thought advisable both by Mother Louise

Margaret and Father Charrier that nothing should be said in the book that would indicate its supernatural origin, and that no mention should be made in it of the proposed Priest's Universal Union. The book was intended for all priests, religious and pious lay people, with, however, the special purpose of preparing the way for the Priest's Universal Union and of serving as a handbook for it when it should be founded. In writing to Father Charrier, who was composing the preface, she said: "Do not put anything in it that would suggest a spiritual origin. If this little book, of which Jesus is the sole Author, makes its way in souls, we shall see about giving more information in subsequent editions."

When the book was completed, it was presented by Monsignor Filipello to His Holiness, Pope Pius X, who had been previously informed of the circumstances under which it was composed. His Holiness replied through his secretary for State, Cardinal Merry del Val, who in a letter to Father Charrier wrote: "*The Holy Father, while praying Our Lord to bless this little book, and crown it with precious fruit, sends the author a special blessing as a pledge of abundant heavenly favors.*"

Besides Cardinal Merry del Val, who wrote on behalf of Pope Pius X, several other Cardinals and Bishops sent their approbation and warmly recommended the book. When the book was finally published, it was well received everywhere. It was translated into most of the European languages during the lifetime of the Author, without her name or anything about the supernatural origin of its contents being known.

She was elected Rev. Mother for a second term in the May after the publication of *The Sacred Heart and the Priesthood*. During this period her bishop, Monsignor Filipello, examined all her writings carefully, questioned her orally and got from her a written statement about their origin. He was convinced that the communications which she received were from Our Lord, and that it was really His wish that a world-wide organization of priests for a more intense propagation of the devotion to the Sacred Heart should be formed. The result of his investigations was that he decided to recommend the foundation of this organization to the Holy See, and ordered her to prepare for him a draft of the statutes according to the lights which she received.

Providence arranged that she should be sent to Rome where everything concerning her writings and her mission was examined into by the Congregation of the Council. The Holy See, without pronouncing

on the supernatural origin of her writings, declared them to be in conformity with the teaching of the Church, and sanctioned the organization for priests and the statutes for it which, by order of her Bishop, she
had drawn up; under the name of "the Priests' Universal Union of the
Friends of the Sacred Heart." She was entrusted with the foundation of
a new monastery of the Visitation which after her death was made an
independent Sisterhood called "Bethany of the Sacred Heart."

When she had completed this foundation, God called her to an early
crown on May 14th, 1915. It had been her desire that she should die
when her mission was completed in order not to be an obstacle to the
spread of the work.

After her death two auxiliary associations were formed according to
her wishes, one for men to cooperate with the priests of the Universal
Union, the other for women to offer their prayers and sacrifices in
union with those of the Sisters of Bethany of the Sacred Heart. Thus
four associations have been formed to promote the work of spreading
devotion to the Sacred Heart of Jesus, branches of which are already
found in most countries of the world. These four branches are:

1) The Priests' Universal Union of the Friends of the Sacred Heart,
intended for all the bishops and priests of the world whether religious
or secular;

2) Bethany of the Sacred Heart, a new Contemplative Order,
the members of which devote themselves to a life of prayer and self-
immolation for priests;

3) The Associates of the Priests' Universal Union composed of
clerical students, Brothers of all Orders, and laymen in the world who
engage to cooperate with the priests of the Priests' Universal Union;

4) The Faithful Friends of Bethany of the Sacred Heart, composed
of Sisters of all Religious Orders, and women living in the world, who
are united to Bethany of the Sacred Heart by a spiritual bond of prayer
and sacrifice for the promotion of the object of the Priests' Universal
Union—to enkindle again in the world the fire of divine love.[2]

The first steps towards having the cause of her canonization intro-
duced have already been taken and an Ecclesiastical Tribunal has been

---

2. For more detailed information about the Priests' Universal Union and its three branches see
    Appendix, page 169.

set up to deal with evidence in its favor. A number of spiritual and temporal favors attributed to her intercession have been published in the Bulletin of the Priests' Universal Union of the Friends of the Sacred Heart.

The Sacred Heart and the Priesthood

Instaurare omnia in Christo. (*Eph.* 1:12).

(PARIS GABRIEL BEAUCHESNE)
119 RUE DE RENNES,   1920.

Visto per delegazione della Curia Vescovile d'Ivrea; nulla osta alla stampa. Nihil obstat.
Collegio Francesa di Botlenga—Ivrea (Prov. de Torino) 10 Marzo 1910.

L. CHOUPIN, S.J.

Letters of Approbation

SEGRETERIA DI STATO,
DI SUA SANTITA.
No. 45032.   DAL VATICANO, July 1st, 1910.

MY REVEREND FATHER,

The Holy Father (Pius X) has received with particular favor the homage of the book entitled *The Sacred Heart and the Priesthood,* furnished with the approval and the encouragement of ecclesiastical authority.

The subject matter of the book is worthy of the deepest interest. It contains an exposition of the sublime relations of intimacy and love between the Heart of Jesus, and the heart of the priest, of the touching harmonies between the Heart of Jesus and the Priesthood; it recounts all that the divine Master has done for those whom He calls "His Friends"; it lays before the priest the necessity of forming his heart and inspiring his life by this ineffable model of the Heart of Jesus.

Sacerdotal souls, as well as souls exercised in the interior life and formed in solid piety will find in these pages edifying and salutary considerations.

The Holy Father, while praying Our Lord to bless this little book and to crown it with precious fruit, sends the author a special blessing as a pledge of abundant heavenly favors.

I unite my sincere thanks for the copy of the book which has been graciously offered to me, and I pray you to accept the expression of my devoted sentiments in Our Lord.

R. CARDINAL MERRY DEL VAL.

SEGRETERIA DI STATO
   DI SUA SANTITA.
N. 193857/SA.

DAL VATICANO, February 15th, 1949

DEAR FATHER O'CONNELL,

I have the honor to convey to you the expression of the Holy Father's cordial gratitude for the copies of your translations of the two books by Mother Louise Margaret Claret de la Touche, namely, "The Book of Infinite Love" and "The Sacred Heart and the Priesthood," which you forwarded some time ago for His acceptance.

His Holiness is well aware that your labors in translating and editing these works in English were motivated by your ardent zeal for the sanctification of priests and for the establishment of the Kingdom of Christ in the hearts of men—that same apostolic zeal which sustained and strengthened you in your long years of devoted toil on the missionfield. It is the Pontiff's earnest prayer that your praiseworthy efforts in that noble cause may be blessed with consoling success, and in pledge of that celestial favor He lovingly imparts to you His paternal Apostolic Benediction.

I gladly avail myself of this occasion to express to you my deep gratitude for the copies of the books which you sent to me. With sentiments of high esteem and cordial regard, I remain,

Yours sincerely in Christ,
J. B. MONTINI.

REV. PATRICK O'CONNELL,
ST. COLUMBAN'S,
NAVAN, CO. MEATH.

To Rev. Father Charrier, S.J.
Bishop's House, Ivrea.   Ivrea, Feb. 2nd, 1910

I have read with genuine satisfaction and, I trust, with special profit for myself, the little volume entitled *The Sacred Heart and the Priesthood.* It contains simple and sober pages which are at the same time vivid and very elevated, full of sweet and strong unction which double its value. For my part, I should be very happy to see this work translated into our language (Italian) and published, for I am persuaded that pious meditation on these pages would be very advantageous to my venerated Confreres in the Priesthood. It will bring them a great abundance of lights, affections and teachings capable of raising them in the knowledge of this divine love with which the Sacred Heart of Jesus is inflamed for His ministers, and it will excite them to a more faithful correspondence with and imitation of this same love.

✠ Matthew,
Bishop of Ivrea

Archbishop's Palace,
Turin.   Turin, April 12th, 1910

The Cardinal Archbishop of Turin joins his prayers to those of His Lordship the Bishop of Ivrea that the divine blessings may descend in abundance on these pious pages, that priests may draw from the reading of this work an increase of faith and love for Jesus Christ in the Blessed Sacrament.

✠ Augustin Card. Richelmy.

Apostolic Chancellery.   Rome, June 30th, 1910

The author of these golden pages is worthy of all praise. They will certainly contribute to keep up solid piety in all the souls who feel the emptiness of worldly ambitions, and they will provide useful instruction for the clergy and will incite them to make themselves always more worthy of the high mission which the Eternal Father has confided to them by His grace.

While occupied in preparing myself for the Eucharistic Congress of

Montreal, I received most opportunely the beautiful book entitled *The Sacred Heart and the Priesthood.* It contains lofty considerations on the infinite love of Jesus for the human race, and the continuation of the work of redemption by means of the Priesthood and the Eucharistic Sacrifice. I believe that I shall have occasion to make use of it at this Congress. What excellent spiritual reading it provides especially for priests . . . . I shall be happy to recommend this dear little book.

✝ VINCENT CARDINAL VANUTELLI.
ROME, June 30th, 1910

To the blessings and congratulations which the author of the beautiful pages: *The Sacred Heart and the Priesthood* has already received, I, very willingly unite my own. At the same time I pray fervently that the sacred ministers of the Altar, by making this book the subject of their pious reading and meditation, may always imitate more closely the sublime example of their divine Master, and that being inflamed with holy and apostolic zeal they may spread on this earth the light of truth and the fire of charity, in which the high mission of the clergy may be summed up.

M. CARDINAL RAMPOLLA

Preface

WE have finally succeeded in realizing one of our dearest desires. When the meditations which we publish today were first communicated to us, we thought that they were destined to serve only for the edification and spiritual advancement of some sacerdotal souls who, having become impregnated with the truths and the light which they contain, would transmit them to the world by word and example.

But some sure friends, priests and religious of different Orders, theologians of value as well as of approved piety, were of the opinion that this light should no longer be left hidden under a bushel. Indeed why deprive our brethren in the priesthood of the consolations and instruction which have come to us through these writings? We have then decided to publish this volume. The sweet doctrine of Infinite Love radiates from each of its pages; it will enlighten the mind and strengthen the will, while warming the heart.

The little book which we present to the public is divided into lectures which might be utilized for the exercises of the month of the Sacred Heart. It would thus furnish excellent meditations for sacerdotal retreats. Candidates for ordination and young priests will find in it precious instruction. . . .

The work comprises three parts. The first part shows us the priest, the creation of Infinite Love, providing for all the spiritual and moral needs of humanity; the second treats of the conformity which the priest should have with Jesus Christ, his Divine Exemplar; the third invites us to meditate on the love of Jesus Christ for His priests, manifesting itself from the first beats of His Sacred Heart and pouring itself out over all time with increasing liberality.

To these three parts some detached pages have been added; meditations on Infinite Love. *This work may be considered as a gift of the Sacred Heart of Jesus to His priests to whom He wishes to reveal the doctrine of Infinite Love.*

What time could be more propitious for this publication? Persecution has broken out on all sides and under every form. The priest is an object of hatred and calumny; Hell is in rage against him and is doing all possible to terrify him, to discourage him and to conquer him.

May these pages be then, in the midst of the tempest, as the voice of Jesus saying to His Apostles: "It is I, be not afraid." (*John* 6:20). Infinite Love is watching over you.

A. CHARRIER, S.J.

APRIL 26TH, 1910

Oratio
Ad Jesum Sacerdotum Aeternum

O JESU, Pontifex aeterne, divine Sacrificator, qui, ineffabili erga homines fratres tuos dilectione impulsus, Sacerdotium christianum e sacratissimo Cordis tui fonte emanare indulsisti, vivificas infiniti Amoris undas in sacerdotum tuorum corda indesinenter fundere velis.

Ipse in eis vivas; eos in Te immutes; sancta tuarum miserationum instrumenta eos gratia tua faciat; in eis et per eos agere ne desinas; divinas virtutes tuas constanter imitantes, et Te semper induentes, in Nomine tuo et in virtute Spiritus tui, eadem quae Tu pro mundi salute operatus es et ipsi operentur.

O divine Redemptor animarum, intuere quanta sit in errorum tenebris dormientium multitudo; infideles pauperculae oves ad os aeternae abyssi pergentes quam multae sint computa; pauperum, esurientium, rudium, debilium, flebiliter derelictorum turbas considera.

Ad nos per tuos sacerdotes redi! Vere Tu in eis semper vivens, per eos operare digneris; per mundum, eorum ope, iterum transiens, doce, condona, solare, sacrifica, et sacra Amoris vincula inter Cor Dei et hominum corda denuo necte. Amen!

Introduction

"*I* AM come to cast fire on the earth," said Jesus Christ, "and what will I but that it be kindled." (*Luke* 12:49).

It is to the priest that Christ has confided the task of spreading abroad and keeping alive the divine fire of Charity; and to render him capable of his sublime mission, He has opened to him, more than to any other, the treasures of His indefectible love. He has united him intimately to Himself by making him participate in His eternal priesthood. The priest is, with Jesus-Priest, pontiff, mediator, advocate, intercessor; he is, with Him, offering, expiation, victim.

From this state of special union with Jesus Christ, all the acts of the priest draw an incomprehensible excellence. The priest, precious gift of Jesus to men, helper chosen by the divine Master to continue on earth His work of love, by his sacerdotal action, labors without intermission to spread everywhere the flames of divine Charity.

In the course of centuries this Charity having grown cold in the world, Jesus Christ resolved to make a new effusion of love in favor of His creatures. He manifested His Heart overflowing with mercy: "Behold," said He, "this Heart which has so loved men!" He invited all, especially those souls paralyzed and frozen by neglect and indifference, to come to this furnace of love that they might find warmth and life.

But it is to priests especially that the Sacred Heart wishes to manifest Itself; to His priests called by Him to rekindle and render operative on earth the fire of His Charity. In His ineffable goodness He deigns to have need of them to do His work. What He could effect directly in souls by His grace, He usually does through the mediation and by the cooperation of His priests.

Ah, if the priest knew the treasures of tender love stored up for him in the Heart of Jesus, with what ardor would he not go and draw from that divine source, to fill himself with love to overflowing! Jesus Christ, by showing His Heart to the world, wishes to warm it, to enlighten it, and to save it. By showing It more intimately to His priests, He wishes to induce them to form their hearts after His, and to identify themselves more and more with Him. He wishes above all to reveal to them

His incomparable love, and by that to inflame them with more ardent charity towards Himself, with more active, more generous and tender devotedness for the salvation of their brethren. He wishes to communicate to His priests a superabundance of divine, supernatural life, in order that they themselves may be able to vivify souls.

That is the plan of Jesus in manifesting His Heart, and those are the thoughts which we wish to express in this humble volume. May these pages strengthen the souls of priests in the love of their sublime vocation, and unite them more than ever to Jesus Christ, the eternal Priest! May they make the faithful who read them have greater confidence in, and more religious and filial respect for, the orders of the sacred hierarchy! May they develop always more and more the knowledge of Infinite Love and the worship of the Sacred Heart of Jesus, King and centre of all hearts!

✢ PART I ✢

The Priest, the Creation of Infinite Love

CHAPTER I

The Priest, the Creation of Infinite Love

*A*LMIGHTY GOD reigned from all eternity in the peaceful possession of His sovereign happiness; but feeling Infinite Love overflow from His being, He willed to create. After drawing incomparable
marvels from nothing by the power of His Word, He formed man, the
king and centre of creation.

Who will ever be able to enumerate the myriad graces which the
Eternal Being, conferred on this privileged creature? Infinite Love
assumed all forms; it was liberal and magnificent like the love of God;
it was tender, delicate and profound like the love of a mother; it was
provident and wise, like the love of a father. Man was enriched with
all gifts, with all graces, with all kinds of beauty. But Infinite Love did
not stop there. It continued to flow with inexaustible profusion on all
creation. In different circumstances it got different names, but it was all
these things at the same time: thus it was a restoring, preserving, vivifying love, a protecting, pardoning, patient love: a love which redeems,
purifies and saves.

And behold! after long ages, the Word of the Father, Incarnate
Love, the Redeemer of the world, Jesus Christ, came on earth. Living
the life of man, He experienced the weakness of man, understood his
wants and restored the work of creation; but above all He loved. He
passionately loved this fallen humanity to which He had intimately
united Himself.

And, one day, He felt Infinite Love overflow from His Heart; and,
wishing to create a being who could continue His work, came to the
relief of man in all his wants; a being who could help man, sustain him,
enlighten him and bring him nearer to God—He created the priest.

To the priest, the creation of the Infinite Love of His heart, Jesus gave a participation in His power; He infused into his heart the devotedness, zeal, goodness and mercy which filled His own. He poured into it humility and purity; He filled it with love; finally, He confided to him four great functions corresponding to the four great needs of the human creature.

1) *Man is profoundly ignorant.* Even after the grace of Baptism, the shadows of original sin still darken his intellect; his personal sins daily intensify these shadows; and his unenlightened mind, plunged in darkness and uncertainty, rushes, almost without noticing it, to eternal perdition. *And the priest teaches.* He gives truth to the human intellect; he shows the way which leads to God; he reveals to souls the luminous horizons of the Faith; his mission is to dispel darkness and to display in all their splendor to every eye these lofty and divine truths which are, with love, the life of the human soul.

2) *Man is a sinner.* The fall of our first parents has left in his nature indelible marks and a strong tendency towards evil; a sort of weakness which makes itself increasingly felt both in his intellectual faculties and in his senses, and in spite of the grace which raises him up, and Infinite Love which draws him from on high, he nevertheless sins again. Being constantly sullied, he has need of being purified again. *And the priest absolves.* Trustee of the Blood of Jesus Christ, the priest applies this divine remedy to the wounds caused by sin; he draws from the infinite treasure of the merits of Jesus Christ, and gives to the purified soul new strength and new help.

3) *Man is unfortunate.* Banished from Heaven, he passes his days on earth in labor and sorrow; suffering presses upon him from every side. Today his body is broken by sickness; tomorrow his heart is rent by treachery or the loss of loved ones; and how often is his soul shaken by fear, remorse or doubt! *But the priest is the consoler.* He makes known to souls the value of suffering; he makes man hope for an eternity of happiness in return for passing sorrow (*2 Cor.* 4:17); he opens the abysses of Infinite Love to afflicted and abandoned hearts; he raises up despairing souls by revealing to them the divine mercies, and, spreading light and love over the earth; he consoles all sorrow and dispels all fear.

4) Finally, *Man cannot do without God.* His weakness must lean on divine strength; his poverty cries out for the treasures of Heaven; his

nothingness has constant need of getting near to the source of all being. And nevertheless, sinner that he is, he shrinks away from divine holiness; God is so great, so pure, so exalted in the inaccessible heights of truth and of justice! A mediator between God and man is needed; that Mediator is Christ, but between Christ and man, so great is man's misery, another mediator is necessary, and *that mediator is the priest.*

And the priest offers sacrifice. He takes the divine Victim in his consecrated hands; he raises Him to Heaven, and God, at this sight, inclines towards the earth; mercy descends; Infinite Love gushes forth more abundantly from the bosom of the Eternal Being. The Creator and His creature are brought together; they have embraced in Christ; they have become united in love.

These are the august functions which the priest exercises for the benefit of man; he teaches, he absolves, he consoles, he offers sacrifice. Jesus, the eternal Priest, had exercised them before him, and with what sublime perfection! He would have wished, if it were possible, to continue exercising them directly by Himself. Nevertheless, it was fitting that Christ, after passing through suffering, should enter into His glory.[3] In His loving mercy He then formed the priest in whom He perpetuates Himself and lives again unceasingly His life of love for men, His brethren. It is by the priest that He continues to instruct, to purify, to console and to bring back again to God all the generations of men that succeed one another on this earth.

In the painful phase through which the world is now passing, poor deluded humanity lured away from God feels more than ever its immense needs. More than ever it demands to be nourished by truth, to be delivered from evil, to be consoled in its sadness, to be brought back to God, and to be warmed by His love.

Jesus Christ should, it would seem, return once more to this earth. But no; His risen Humanity can remain in its glory. He has provided for all the needs of man; He has left him the Blessed Eucharist and His priesthood.

By the Blessed Eucharist, man can nourish his soul on eternal Truth and infinite Love, and, in a manner, divinize his weak flesh and his senses inclined to sin. In the priesthood, he can find those helps which

---

3.   *Luke* 24:26.

are continually necessary for him in the course of his life of misery and trials.

Though in the Blessed Eucharist Jesus is always the same, eternally living, in the priest, His divine life varies in intensity, not that He does not give Himself with equal abundance to all, but because the priest draws more or less from this abundance. In order that Jesus may live again in the priest, it is necessary that the priest live by Jesus.

Infinite Love pouring itself forth from the divine Being created man; this same love, issuing from the Heart of Jesus, has created the priest; and just as man can find his true life and perfection only by returning to God, his eternal principle, so it is only by going to the Heart of Jesus that the priest can attain to the plenitude of life and the perfection of his sacerdotal being. That is the reason why, at this hour when the holy functions of the priesthood are so necessary to the world, Jesus calls His priests to His Heart. It is in order that they may draw new graces from this divine source and, by immersing themselves again in this ocean from which they have come forth, they may find a renewal and an increase of sacerdotal life.

Oh, let the priest go to Jesus, let him keep near Him; the priest whose mission is so great and whose action can be so fruitful! Let him consider the actions of this divine model, let him listen to His words, let him penetrate into His thoughts, let him follow Him step-by-step in the holy Gospel, let him learn from this adorable Master how to perform worthily the sacred functions of the priesthood. Jesus has exercised these functions before him; the priest has only to follow His divine footprints. To be clothed with Christ means to imitate Christ, to reproduce His adorable virtue, His holy actions, even His divine gestures. And if anyone ought to be clothed with Christ, is it not above all the priest whose duty it is to give Christ to the world?

✝ Prayer for Priests

O, Jesus eternal High Priest, divine Offerer of Sacrifice, Who, in an incomparable transport of love for men, Thy brethren, didst allow the Christian priesthood to issue from Thy Sacred Heart, deign to continue to pour out on Thy priests the life-giving streams of Infinite Love.

Live Thou in them, transform them into Thyself; render them by

Thy grace the instruments of Thy mercies; act in them and through them, and grant, that, having been completely clothed with Thee by the faithful imitation of Thy adorable virtues, they may perform in Thy Name and by the strength of Thy Spirit, the works which Thou Thyself hast accomplished for the salvation of the world.

Divine Redeemer of souls, see how great is the multitude of those who still sleep in the darkness of error; count the number of those unfaithful sheep that are walking on the edge of the eternal abyss; consider the crowds of the poor, the hungry, the ignorant and the weak, who are groaning in their state of abandonment. Return to us by Thy priests, live again in very truth in them; act through them and pass again through the world teaching, pardoning, consoling, offering sacrifice, renewing the sacred bonds of love between the Heart of God and the hearts of men. Amen.[4]

---

4. Indulgences: 300 days once a day. A plenary indulgence on usual conditions, if recited daily for a month. (Pius X Rescript in his own hand March 3, 1905. *Raccolta* 1937).

SECOND LECTURE

Jesus Teaching

*A*FTER a long and silent preparation of thirty years Jesus began to teach. He possessed in Himself the plenitude of all knowledge; His human intellect, expanded and perfected by its union with the divine intellect, embraced the vast expanse of the most sublime knowledge, and penetrated into the heart of things in their minutest detail. The marvellous harmony of the faculties of His soul and of the sentiments of His Heart, the perfect equilibrium which reigned in His whole being, regulated the course of His thoughts, and, without having need of working to instruct Himself like other men, He possessed, without effort, knowledge in His intellect, as He had, without limit, love stored up in His Heart.

Though the world was awaiting the lessons from His divine lips in order to be born again to life and light, nevertheless Jesus allowed thirty years to pass by without manifesting His sublime wisdom. Why this long wait? Why deprive humanity so long of the celestial lights which were to dispel the darkness of its ignorance? Let us not forget that Jesus is our model. He knew that man requires long work and painful efforts to acquire those treasures of knowledge necessary for the instruction of souls, and He wished to give His priests an example of a slow and serious preparation.

If it is question of profane teaching, it suffices to have knowledge and to know how to teach. But when it is necessary to give God to souls and to give souls to God, the cultivation of the intellect will no longer suffice. The entire man must be transformed; he himself must pass through a succession of trials, and at least begin to acquire this experimental knowledge of suffering, of weakness, and of the miseries of humanity which he must possess to instruct and enlighten his brethren.

Doubtless, before his thirtieth year the priest may occupy himself with this first function of his ministry. But then, he will require to have prudence, distrust in himself and humble recourse to others for light and guidance. It is above all to his divine Master that the priest should go to receive instruction. Let him then study this sublime Teacher of souls, let him train himself to speak like Him, and teach like Him.

When Jesus, leaving the seclusion of His hidden life, began to reveal the treasures of knowledge which He bore within Himself, the whole world was plunged in the darkness of error. Paganism and the crimes which it engenders flourished everywhere, and even among the chosen people, truth began to be enveloped in a pall of darkness. The Jews, who, up to that time had kept intact the deposit of divine truth, seemed on the point of losing it. The Synagogue was being rent asunder into numerous sects; love of riches and ambition for honors had little by little broken down the wall which separated Israel from the idolatrous nations surrounding her. By the perfidious insinuations of a lying philosophy, under the pressure of enervating sensualism and by giving free rein to the passions, the sons of Abraham felt their faith totter and saw the light being extinguished in their hands.

At that precise moment Jesus appeared. He, the Uncreated Word, the Light of light, 'True God of True God, came to bring Truth to the earth, absolute Truth without mixture, without shadow, such as it is in God and in His eternal day, in its divine clearness, in its sovereign exactness. He came to rekindle the torch of Justice and Truth, without which humanity can only go astray in the march through time. He came, with all the authority of His divine Wisdom, to teach the rights of God and the duties of man, the mercies of God and the miseries of man; in fine, to restore order in the human intellect deranged by the errors of paganism.

The sinful woman of Samaria was, one day, to say to Jesus Himself: "I know that the Messias cometh (who is called Christ): therefore, when He is come, He will tell us all things." (*John* 4:25). This was indeed the great mission of the Saviour; to instruct souls! His teaching was universal. On all subjects, in all matters, He brought the light of truth. He combated all the errors of that time, and refuted, in advance, those which the disordered activity of human thought was to give birth to in the future. By the example of His life, and afterwards by

His words, He taught what man could know about God. He revealed Him as the powerful Creator, infinitely holy and sovereignly just; but above all He revealed Him as a *Father* ineffably good and infinitely merciful.

Dogma, moral principles, the relations of man with God and with his fellow-man; the great principles which should rule the family and society, and direct the human conscience on the shadowy path of this earthly life, were all lighted by the brilliant rays of the truth of Jesus. He neglected no occasion to instruct the people: "All were mute with admiration at His teaching, for He spoke as one having authority." (*Matt.* 7:28–29, *Mark* 1:22, *Luke* 4:32).

Indeed how many times did not this adorable Master, so sober and so measured in His words, repeat: "Verily, verily I say to you." "We speak what we know and We give testimony of what We have seen" (*John* 3:11), declares He. He is indeed the Master, the infallible teacher of truth. Thus, raising His voice under the porticoes of the Temple, could He justly cry: "I am the way, the truth and the life," "he that followeth Me, walketh not in darkness." (*John* 14:6, 8:12). Later, on the day of His sorrowful Passion, standing in the middle of the Pretorium, He replied to Pilate with incomparable majesty: "For this was I born and for this came I into the world: that I should give testimony to the truth. Everyone that is of truth, heareth My voice." (*John* 18:37). This voice of Jesus, so humble and so sweet, resounded for but three years in a little corner of the world, privileged among all. Few men heard it; what it taught, in opposition to the ideas till then current, seemed folly and madness and nevertheless . . . it was Truth. And Truth always remains; in the end it will always triumph over falsehood. It will never perish, for it is born of God and like Him is immortal.

Truth! Behold what after Jesus, what with Jesus, the priest should give to the world. But in order to teach it, in order to communicate it to others, he must himself possess it, and in order to possess it he must go to its divine source and draw it from there; he must go to his divine Master and seek it from Him. When the priest receives his mission to teach, he receives at the same time an abundance of heavenly light which he should develop in himself. He must consolidate, he must guard intact the deposit of truth which he has received. Considering the many errors by which he is surrounded, it is only with much labor and conflict that he will succeed in defending it and preserving it in its integrity.

The truth of God is immutable and cannot change. Holy Church possesses it in its entirety. If among the events and the vicissitudes of time it seems to change, it is only an appearance. The human intellect, according as it is more or less pure, grasps its meaning more or less clearly. Truth can increase and develop, or on the contrary, it can dwindle away in the intellect of man, but in itself, it is one and unchangeable. It can make itself more precise, it can be more firmly established, it can be defined and explained, and that is the justification of the slow but incessant development of the truths taught by the Church. Really new truths, especially truths in contradiction with the original truth, cannot exist.

The Priest Instructing Souls

The priest, then, to conserve intact the divine truth poured by Jesus into his soul on the day of his Ordination, must strengthen it against the attacks of error. These attacks come to him from three sides at the same time. In the first place, Satan, the evil spirit, the eternal fomenter of discord and hatred, who seeks to destroy truth everywhere that he can find it, endeavors to snatch it from the heart of the priest, from the priest who is his enemy, always alert in the struggle against his infernal wiles. In the second place, the spirit of the world and its maxims tend incessantly to weaken truth, and the priest lives in the midst of the world; he breathes the air of falsehood and is unconsciously affected by the softening influence of its false doctrines. In the third place, in fine, in himself, in these depths in which original sin has left its trace, what seeds of error exist in a latent state! The smallest breath of pride is sufficient to awaken them to life, the least contamination can make them fertile.

To triumph over these multiple enemies, the priest has three weapons at hand, three powerful weapons which always assure victory. The first is union with holy Church, inviolable attachment to the Holy See, the infallible organ of truth. What can the machinations of Satan effect against the unshakable rock on which the Church is founded? Can we have any fear that he who walks with Peter will go astray? With Peter to whom the Master has said: "I have prayed for thee that thy faith fail not: and thou being once converted confirm thy brethren." (*Luke* 22:32).

The priest will triumph over the spirit of the world by union with Christ, the conqueror of the world; by a union produced by the spirit of prayer, by the study of the Heart of Jesus and His adorable virtues; by a complete separation, interior but real, from all that Jesus reproves and condemns in the world.

But to triumph over himself, to annihilate in himself every source of error, to become inaccessible to lies and firm against every attack, to possess with security the treasure of truth and keep it always intact, the priest has to be rooted and grounded in humility. A holy and just distrust of himself, of his own judgments a ready recourse to others for light, a humble submission of faith are what he needs to remain true, to fortify himself against the illusions of false science; to be, in a word, like John, "a burning and a shining light" to enlighten the people, to be, with Jesus, "the light of the world."

Jesus taught truth to all, great and little, poor and rich, children and old men. From the Prince of priests to the poor Samaritan woman, all were instructed by His word, all received the truth from His divine lips. With marvellous flexibility of intellect and incomparable humility, He could always bring Himself down to the level of those whom He was instructing.

With Nicodemus, "a master in Israel," He is profound, sublime, He sounds the depths of the greatest mysteries; with the priests and the scribes, His teaching is always based on the law, the prophets and the Holy Scripture; with the people, He is simple and familiar, He expresses Himself by comparisons taken from the works of the fields, and these are His divine parables: the sower, the mustard-seed, the vine, etc. He always adapts Himself to His hearers; but He is never vulgar, never affected, never difficult to understand, even in the most sublime matters. What charm in this teaching of Jesus, so clear, so simple, so rich in heavenly doctrine and so free from superfluous ornament! What sweet majesty in His smallest words! What affable gravity, what modest dignity, what persuasive force, what clearness of exposition and what grace! What impressive and sublime poetry in those comparisons taken from nature!

Oh, if we could study in detail the ineffable charms of our adorable

Master! He is the Word of the Eternal Father; He is the divine Master descended from Heaven to instruct souls. When we say this, have we not said everything? On the priest too is laid the responsibility of expounding truth to all. If he would be truly an apostle, truly the priest of Christ, he must make himself like Jesus, all things to all men. His sole aim should be to communicate the truth which he possesses and the love which consumes him.

Far then from addressing himself to a particular class, from seeking new methods suitable only to certain individuals and interesting only to the few, let him endeavor to bring himself down to the level of his audience. Always clear, always exact, let him preach the truth simply, with the sole intention of doing it well. He will then have found the secret of that penetrating unction which comes from the heart, and with which the twofold love of Jesus and of souls touches naturally the lips of the priest. In his teaching, he must give the very best of himself, and without despising anyone, he must give himself entirely to his sublime mission of instructor of souls.

THIRD LECTURE

Difficulties of Teaching

*I*N HIS PUBLIC MISSION, when teaching, Jesus met with many obstacles, many difficulties, much suffering. He had infinite patience. He did not allow Himself to be discouraged either by the coarseness of His hearers, or by their slowness of comprehension, or by their groundless objections. The criticisms, the insults, the double-dealing of those whom He sought to instruct and enlighten, could not succeed in wearying Him. He never had His own glory in view. He did not seek human success. He sowed the divine seed in souls with full hands and with full heart, and He left to the Spirit of love the care of making it germinate and of bringing it to maturity.

He knew that by teaching His moral code, sweet, it is true, but nevertheless austere, He would turn many away. He knew by His divine foreknowledge that many of those whom He was instructing would either allow the seeds of life to perish in themselves through negligence, or that they would even tear them out with their own hands. Nevertheless, He continued to give His divine lessons, and to open to all the treasures of His Wisdom.

Contradictions, contempt, difficulties of all kinds are met with by the priest in his work. He must not let himself be cast down. Is not Jesus, the divine Master, with him? Has he not the divine promises of Jesus to comfort and sustain him? Let him then take up the cross of His Master and proceed with his work.

But let him take care not to water down the Gospel (*2 Tim.* 4:2–4) under pretext of reconciliation between the spirit of the world and the spirit of Christ; let him take care not to make a Christianity of his own imagination in order to flatter human passions. The Gospel truths of themselves will make their impression on souls; the priest has only to show them as they are, lighted up by divine reflections of the sweetness and mercy of the Heart of Jesus. Yes, let him point out clearly the rights of God, His just, strong laws; let him tell about His patience, His long-suffering, and the ineffable love of the Redeemer of souls; but let him never descend to base compromises, to worldly modes of action and to culpable seeking after personal success.

"Behold, I send you as sheep in the midst of wolves; be then prudent as serpents and simple as doves!" (*Matt.* 10:16; *Luke* 10:3). These are the words which Jesus addresses to His Apostles, to His priests, when sending them to announce the good news. And how marvelously He Himself, our adorable Master, has succeeded in uniting simplicity and prudence in His teaching! When He instructed souls individually how prudently He acted! He advanced by degrees, having patience with their weakness, demanding from each only what he was able to give, waiting with infinite patience until the soul should open itself to grace and respond to the overtures of His Mercy. He prepared minds slowly and gently before revealing to them the truth; He encouraged the faint-hearted; He never forced His doctrine rudely on others.

And in His public teaching, what prudence He displayed! Jesus always showed Himself respectful to legitimate authority; the friend of peace, He knew how to baffle by His wisdom the cunning attacks of His enemies; and, after three years of preaching during which He had taught a doctrine and given laws completely opposed to those of the world, no witness was found who could give evidence against Him when He was accused before the Judges and the Princes.

When He stigmatized vice or exposed errors to view, He never named the culprits. What exquisite discretion He displayed in His conduct towards the adulterous woman! What reserve in His words when He has to instruct the common people in the most delicate precepts of morality, when He reveals to souls the sanctity of the marriage-bond, or the divine charms of virginity! His prudence on this point is so great, His words are so chaste that the child of most innocent soul and most unconscious of evil can read and re-read His Gospel without anything troubling its mind or casting a shadow over it.

Let the priest, then, after the example of the Master, combine prudence with simplicity in his teaching. If he wishes to do good in the midst of the corrupt world in which he lives, he must speak and act with divine wisdom. Let him be prudent in his public preaching, let him be more apostle than controversialist, let him be much more the dispenser of the gifts of God and minister of mercy, than the violent reformer of the world.

Hatred is only conquered by love. (*Rom.* 8:28). Sin was destroyed only by the blood of Jesus, who was meek and humble of heart! It is necessary at times, no doubt, to be strong; but prudence must regulate strength, must moderate the rigors of justice, must direct the action which punishes as well as the action which pardons.

Let the priest be prudent in his private instruction. Let him study souls well before giving directions; let him be prudent when he is deciding their vocation; prudent when he is making them contract bonds which may determine their future, and perhaps trouble their conscience.

Let the priest be prudent above all in the instructions which he gives to young girls and women; they themselves are too often imprudent! How many families are unsettled, how many married couples have their harmony disturbed, how many souls, given a wrong direction, and sometimes driven away from the path of piety, by counsel imprudently given, by words that are, doubtless, just and holy in their real sense, but capable of being misunderstood on account of their form.

Let the priest of Jesus wrap himself in the mantle of prudence after the example of his divine Model. He also is a teacher, a teacher of souls; he is a teacher of sanctity and virtue. Let his words then be an echo of the words of Jesus which were all impregnated with wisdom, with moderation, and with truth.

FOURTH LECTURE

Teaching by Example

O UR adorable Master did not confine Himself to teaching by words, to teaching by public preaching and private instruction; He taught above all by example. "He first did," says Holy Scripture, "and then He taught." (*Acts.* 1:1). Is not the best lesson the lesson by example? What the ear cannot be always hearing, the eye can see, and is not the impression received through the eye, the stronger and the more vivid? Is not the heart more easily inflamed by having seen than by having heard? Jesus knew this; that is why, when He came to the teaching of the virtues, He commenced by practicing them all. He made them appear in Himself so beautiful, so desirable, so fascinating, that hearts became inflamed with the desire of possessing them.

And even now, is it not the recollection of the sublime virtues which He practiced on earth that moves us to imitate them? Is it not the thought of His divine patience that makes us patient, of His humility that makes us accept humiliation? Is it not the example of His adorable purity and that of His Virgin Mother, more than the few short words that He has said about it, which we find related in the Gospel, that causes the flower of virginity to bloom in all lands?

Our poor nature had been so profoundly affected by original sin that the words of Jesus, the words of the Word Incarnate, all powerful though they are, would not have been able, perhaps, to transform souls so promptly, if Our Saviour had not added to them His divine example.

Jesus Christ Himself first carried out all that He demanded of regenerated man in the way of virtue and sanctity. He carved out the way, He walked in it Himself, drawing after Him souls of good will. He placed Himself as a model before humanity, before this deformed and diseased humanity which had long lost the divine resemblance, and He said to it: "Look at Me and reproduce on the canvas of your soul My divine lineaments." Jesus washed this canvas in His blood and made it white. The Church came and seeing man weak and incapable, maternally took his hand and guided the brush. And behold! soon copies of the divine Model appeared. Some of them bore such a close resemblance, were so conformable to the original, that the Heavenly Father recognized in them His divine Son. (*Rom.* 8:29). They were the saints formed after the example of Jesus, nourished by His word and living His life.

As in the case of Jesus Christ, it is above all by his example that the priest must teach. He ought therefore to be a living copy of Christ, he ought always to present to the world this divine image. Let him then offer in himself a finished model of virtue, a living and visible model, easy to imitate. Being a man, weak like other men, although raised by grace above the miseries and baseness of the earth, he must, by his example, help other men, his brethren, to rise even to the height of Christ.

"Let your modesty," says the Apostle to the faithful, "appear before all men." (*Philip* 4:5). What then is modesty? It is the transparent veil which moderates the light of two sublime virtues, humility and purity, without hiding them; it is their most fragrant perfume which insinuates itself into hearts, draws them and transforms them; it is the most sweet odor of humility and purity. If the Apostle recommended this modesty to the faithful, how much more should he demand it of priests!

This divine virtue shone in the countenance and in the whole outward demeanor of Christ; it flowed from His profound humility and from His adorable purity. Let it be also the ornament of the priest; let it envelop him on every side, let it mingle itself with all his actions, let it be found in all his words, let it accompany him in the exercise of his priestly duties, and he will be a living sermon of the truth and the virtues of Jesus.

Everything in the priest should instruct, everything should edify. Placed as a connecting link between Jesus and souls, he ought to lead them in his own person to His Divine Master, and unite them to Him. Souls should ascend to Jesus by means of the priest. The words of the priest, his actions, the purity, humility and self-sacrifice of his life, ought to be as powerful levers to lift up souls, as serene lights to guide them to God!

Prayer

O, Christ, ineffable light, divine fire of uncreated truth, come and enlighten our minds! Thou art the Word of the Father, the splendor of His glory, the light of the world, come and dispel the darkness which clouds our horizon! Thou dost always speak. Thou dost always instruct in the person of priests. May Thy light come to us by Thy priests; and, as it is by their hands that we receive Thy adorable body, may it also be from their lips that we receive Thy truth! So strengthen them in the possession of justice and truth that they may never fail in Thy way. Unite them so intimately to Thee, that they may think only Thy thoughts, that they may teach only Thy wisdom. Unite them so closely among themselves, that they may be made strong against the assaults of sin. Fill their minds with Thy light and their hearts with Thy chaste love, in order that, in their turn, they may enlighten all the souls that Thou has confided to them. Amen.

CHAPTER III

FIFTH LECTURE

Jesus Pardoning

"GOD is love." (*1 John* 4:8). His life is love; all His divine movements, whether within, or without, are movements of love. If He engenders in His bosom, it is His Word, the sublime word of love which He says to Himself. If the beauty and excellence of His Son delight Him and provoke a movement of love, and if His Son, at the same time, enraptured with love for His Father, makes a similar movement, the Holy Spirit proceeds from it, the sigh of love breathed forth by the Father and the Son.

All that God has created outside of Himself is a creation of love, for He creates only to love, and all the movements which He makes towards His creatures are also movements of love. Whether He orders, forbids, punishes, pardons, favors or reproves, it is always love.

But this ineffable love, according as He exercises it, takes different names: when love commands, it is power; when it favors, it is goodness; when it punishes, it is justice; when it pardons, it is mercy. Thus love always lives, always acts in God, and although it assumes different forms, it is a unique love, a unique action, a unique power: it is God in His Unity, absolute, immense, profound, without limit, incommensurable, eternal.

Man was therefore created by love, by a fertile, abundant, liberal love which felt the need of pouring itself out; the love of a Father who wishes to communicate His life; the love of an artist who wishes to produce masterpieces. This love of predilection fills the guiltless man with its gifts. When man had sinned, the love which chastises, Justice, was about to exercise its rigor, but the love which pardons, Mercy, was there to arrest the arm that was raised to strike.

The divine Word, engendered by love, living in the bosom of love,

Love itself, offered Himself to pay the debt of the guilty. He took the form of love which pardons, and, during a long chain of centuries, this merciful love raised itself like a rampart in the very bosom of God to preserve sinful man from the thunderbolts of outraged justice.

And after humanity had long suffered and wept, after it had finally awakened the pity of God by successive calamities, and by long centuries of waiting, the Word descended on the earth. He clothed Himself with our flesh; He assumed our weakness and our mortality: He was our Christ, our Jesus!

He, ineffable Love, incarnate Mercy, came not only to teach truth, not only to enlighten the human intellect by His divine lights, but above all, He came to bring to earth the pardon of God, to wash away with His own blood the iniquities of the world, to break the chains which held the souls of men captive in the bonds of sin. Jesus was Himself this great Pardon of God, substantial and living Pardon, efficacious and saving Pardon! Must one then be astonished when we say that the tendency of Jesus was towards mercy; that the *supernatural movement, natural to His Heart,* was always to pardon and absolve?

If we follow the divine Master attentively during the three years of His Public Life, if we keep close to His steps during the time of His apostolate, so laborious and so fruitful, we shall see Him ceaselessly engaged in search of sinners, continually occupied in breaking the bonds of iniquity which enslave souls. Jesus will say: "God has sent His Son into the world, not to judge the world, but that the world may be saved by Him." (*John* 3:17).

Oh, how He will fulfill His mission of Saviour! How ardent He will be in seeking out souls! How lovingly He will incline to the aid of the sinner in his deepest misery, to raise him up to a divine holiness!

Jesus loves these sinners whom He wishes to pardon. And nevertheless what are sinners before God? They are His mortal enemies! They are first of all ungrateful ones: they have received everything from God, and despising His divine liberality, they have forgotten His goodness, and have trampled on His Heart. They are also rebels: though obliged by their state as creatures to be docile and submissive to God, they have nevertheless shaken off the yoke of His authority, so legitimate and so sweet, and have constituted themselves sole masters. But they are traitors: the government of the world had been entrusted to them;

they should have watched over all the inferior creatures and led them to God, but, betraying the divine trust, they have turned these creatures from their end, forcing them, in a manner, to abandon their Master, their Creator and their King.

And Jesus loves them—these sinners! Yes, He loves them. It was His love for them that made Him descend from Heaven and come on earth to work, to suffer, and to die in pain and ignominy.

Now that He has come upon this earth, soon to be watered by His blood, see how He willingly seeks the company of sinners, how He converses with them, how He welcomes with joy all those who present themselves to Him. He is so often in their midst and treats them so kindly that the jealous Pharisees say to His disciples: "Why doth your Master eat with publicans and sinners?" (*Matt.* 9:11). They take occasion of His merciful goodness to deny His divine mission: "If He were a prophet," they said in the bitterness of their egoistic and compassionless hearts, "He would know surely who and what manner of woman this is that toucheth Him, that she is a sinner." (*Luke* 7:39). How far from knowing Jesus those people were who thought that misery could repel Him, and that a sinner that weeps was unworthy of His mercy!

There is a saying of Jesus, adorable in its simplicity and its depth, which reveals to us in a few words both the all-merciful inclination of His Heart, and the divine mission which His Father had entrusted to Him to pardon and absolve: "I am come," He one day said, "to seek and save that which was lost." (*Luke* 19:10). Indeed, it is not only to receive those who would come to Him, to welcome repentant sinners and pardon them, that He came among us; it is to go to meet them, to seek out everywhere these poor creatures whom sin has rendered blind, or shame keeps back, or cowardice enslaves.

During these three years of apostolate He will do nothing else but search for souls! He will, day in day out, trudge through the towns and villages of Judea and Galilee. He will direct His barque towards all the shores of the lake of Genesareth; He will penetrate into the depths of the deserts; He will pass over the pagan lands of Tyre and Sidon; He will go along the banks of the Jordan and the shores of the sea; at the peril of His life, He will go and mix with the great crowds come to Jerusalem for the festivals; He will frequent the porticoes of the Temple where the doctors dispute, the arcades of the Probatic pool where the sick are crowded together. Nothing will repel Him in His searching; nothing will tire His indefatigable desire of finding souls to save. This ardent passion for the salvation of souls carries Jesus beyond Himself: it multiplies His human strength tenfold; it makes Him undertake numberless works, until it finally brings Him to the Pretorium and to Golgotha!

He whom Jesus has chosen to continue His life on earth, this privileged one whom a participation in the anointing of the Christ-Saviour makes also a saviour and liberator of souls, the priest, ought to have in his heart this ardent flame, this vehement desire, this holy passion for the salvation of his brethren. Invested by the divine Master with this sublime power of pardoning and absolving, he ought to desire nothing more than to be able to use it; and with generous ardor, he should, by the aspirations and desires of his heart, go in search of souls and, if necessary, undertake long and dangerous journeys by land and sea.

He should attempt everything to save souls: he should forget himself, sacrifice his personal views, absolutely spurn all desire of repose and enjoyment. Did Jesus spare His strength and His time? On the contrary, did He not consume both entirely? Did He not give Himself completely? Did He dream of earthly joys, of a peaceful life, of assured tranquillity? Did He believe that He could be Saviour by sparing Himself, or that He could give abundant life to many without delivering up and losing His own life? (*Matt.* 16:24–25; *Luke* 9:23–24).

The priest of Jesus, the heir to the sentiments of his divine Master, has a great heart and an ardent soul. An indefatigable gleaner, he wishes to gather innumerable sheaves of souls in order to present them to God; he wishes to pour out divine pardons in abundance. What cares he if the sun scorches him, if the sweat bathes his tired body! He knows that when the evening of life shall come, when the hour for work shall have ceased, he will find in the Heart of the Master refreshment ineffably sweet!

SIXTH LECTURE

Magdalen and Zacheus

WHILE our divine Saviour was passing along in search of souls to pardon and absolve, He met different kinds of people on His way. Some, like Magdalen, came to Him of their own accord. A disgust for sin had, one day, taken possession of Magdalen. An inward grace had moved her heart to return to God: a word of Jesus, heard, as if by chance, had conquered her last resistance. She had come and thrown herself at the feet of the Master. In the midst of her tears, she made the humiliating confession of her faults. Filled with sorrow, but also with confidence, she had remained there pressing with her lips the divine feet of the Saviour, and waiting for the absolution that was to loose her chains, the pardon which was to make her forever the happy conquest of Infinite Love.

Our adorable Master had recognized in her a chosen soul, one of those ardent souls whom pleasure may fascinate for a few moments, but for whom earthly loves are too cold, too unstable, and of too short duration. Their hearts, attracted by Infinite Love, but ignorant of the way that leads to it, sometimes allow themselves to be deceived by the mirage of human affections; they sink little by little to the lowest depths, but they cannot remain there. It was thus with Magdalen. She, the sister of Martha and Lazarus, carried away by her heart, had forgotten the holy traditions of her race and the example of her own people; she had fallen into sin, bringing sorrow and shame on her family. But her soul was too noble to find its happiness in evil; her heart was too great to be contented with the love of creatures; she was to belong to Christ, and Christ conquered her!

What sweet emotion penetrated the Heart of Jesus when He saw before him the soul, fallen it is true, but which a single word was to raise up to Him; this soul which His pardon was to make again so beautiful! Already He sees admirable virtues in her. She has faith, because of her own accord she comes to ask for pardon; hope, boundless confidence keeps her at the feet of the Master; love has subjugated and conquered her. What more is necessary? The ineffable words of Jesus: "Thy sins are forgiven thee" (*Matt.* 9:2), came as a reply to the tears and to the loving confidence of Mary.

And afterwards, the Master does not abandon her. He continues to instruct her. He sometimes demands from her heroic acts. He leads her slowly towards eternal happiness, from Magdala to Bethany, from Bethany to Calvary, from Calvary to Heaven. Even after the Resurrection, He makes her practice self-denial; He forbids her to touch Him (*John* 20:17) and later He permits her to suffer in the persecutions at Jerusalem. He made of this sinner a miracle of love. She will be the saint, the lover, the beloved of His Heart, and this will be the work of His merciful pardon!

Among the souls that the Master met with, others, like Zacheus, had committed sin by following the broad and easy road traced by the spirit of the world. The rich publican of Jericho, who had attained wealth by means more or less just, enjoyed the pleasures of life without scruple or remorse. A secret grace, however, had awakened in his soul something like a vague desire to lead a better life. But this had only been a fugitive thought on which the urgency of his business and the cares of his great property did not permit him to dwell. The rumor of the miracles of Jesus has, however, reached him, and suddenly he learns that the great Prophet is soon going to enter his town. Curiosity, which he imagines to be quite natural, but which, in truth, is nothing else but a beneficent touch of grace, urges him to desire to see Christ. He is not eager to speak to Him; he has nothing to say to Him, it seems to him; he only wants to see Him, to consider this extraordinary Man whose name is, on everyone's lips, and whom the people acclaim.

The criticisms and contempt of the Jews had not troubled Zacheus in his luxurious and easy life; nor does human respect stop him when he makes up his mind to see Jesus. He climbs up one of those sycamore trees planted in the long avenue of Jericho, and there awaits the passing of the Master.

While Zacheus contemplates Him as He advances slowly accompanied by the crowds, he suddenly feels the eyes of Jesus fixed on him. This look, profound and sweet, and radiating light, which penetrates him to the depths of his soul, moves him strangely; and behold! he hears himself called by name: "Zacheus," says Jesus with infinite sweetness, "make haste and come down: for this day I must abide at your house." (*Luke* 19:5). In his house! He can hardly persuade himself that he has heard aright. Overwhelmed to the inmost depths of his soul by this condescension of the Master, he can find no words to reply. He runs to his house, he gives his orders, he makes all preparations. He wishes that Jesus find with him generous and magnificent hospitality.

Soon, the Son of David, the great Prophet of Israel, still followed by the crowd, presents Himself at the gate of his sumptuous dwelling. He enters. What passed then in the soul of Zacheus? A vivid light shows him the injustice of his life. The goodness of Jesus, who has deigned to choose him as his host, in spite of the general contempt of which he is the object, appears to him so merciful and so sweet, that his heart is profoundly touched by it. At the sight of Christ, poorly clad, living on alms, going about doing good, diffusing light and peace, with serene countenance, His eyes always filled with mercy and His hand always raised to bless, the rich publican understands the vanity of the deceitful riches in which up to then he had placed his happiness. He understands that his soul is made for something greater, for something better and more useful.

Standing before the Master, whom he has installed as King in his house, Zacheus with a large heart and a will fully bent on good, said: "Behold, I give the half of all my goods to the poor, and if I have wronged anyone of anything, I restore him fourfold." (*Luke* 19:8). He does not say that he will give, he gives; it is already done in his will; and if he has committed acts of injustice (and how easy it is to commit them when the love of riches dominates the heart), if he has committed acts of injustice, he repairs them generously.

What joy for Jesus when He sees Zacheus responding so faithfully to His grace! His merciful looks will not then have been fixed in vain on this soul! His advances all full of love will not this time be repulsed! Considering the sublime work operated by His mercy, the divine Master cries out: "This day is salvation come to this house." (*Luke* 19:9). And directing anew His penetrating look into the intimate depths of this soul regenerated by His love, He says: "He is indeed also a son of Abraham." Then He adds these beautiful words, which are a splendid and a divine summary of His own life: "For the Son of man is come to seek and to save that which was lost." (*Luke* 19:10).

The Samaritan Woman

*J*ESUS did not, however, always meet such easy conquests on His way. He must sometimes wait very long at the gate of souls, He must weary Himself in pursuit of them. He must battle with their opposition. We see an example of this in the conversation with the Samaritan woman.

The Master, in His divine foreknowledge, had seen in the town of Sichar many souls to be saved. In the midst of them, He had discerned a sinful woman and, in His mercy, He had resolved not only to draw her away from evil, but even to make her the apostle of her fellow-citizens. Very often, He had taken the humble form of a suppliant before His Father; very often, He had sent His grace into this guilty soul, which was still closed to the sweet influence of His love. One day, however, the Master decided to make a final assault, and with His disciples He took the road to Samaria.

He was approaching Sichar. The midday sun was beating down on the plain, gilding on the horizon the stately brow of Gazarim. The corn, still green, trembled beneath the gusts of wind. On the edge of the road, the fountain of the Patriarch stood out white under the shade of the palm trees; Jesus was wearied and stopped to rest. He allowed His disciples to continue their journey towards the town, and He went and sat down, pensive and sad, beside the well of Jacob.

O divine weakness, O adorable weariness of Jesus, how mysterious you are! Doubtless it was not alone the fatigue of the road that thus overcame Him. He, the Victim of Love, voluntarily laden with the sins of the world, sometimes felt Himself sink under their weight. The long resistance of the woman of Sichar, the feeling which He had of the struggles of so many other souls against the efforts of His mercy, threw Him into profound sadness. His Heart, filled with love, throbbed sorrowfully, and His delicate body was weary to exhaustion.

Soon, He saw coming towards Him her whose salvation had already cost Him so many sighs and tears. How much still remained to be done in this soul to bring it to repentance! The erroneous doctrines on which she had been nourished from her infancy in this land of Samaria, where some shreds of Divine Revelation were mingled with the grossest idolatry; the various influences exercised on her by those men to whom she had successively given herself, had warped her mind and corrupted her judgment. A character that was tenacious, argumentative, given to raillery; a sensuous nature, opposed to work and effort, were so many obstacles to her return to good; Jesus, however, did not let Himself be discouraged. This Physician of souls did not come for those who were well but for those that were sick. (*Matt.* 9:12). He is the resurrection and the life of the body and the soul, and decides to use His divine power in resuscitating this woman's soul, which He clearly sees to be dead to the life of grace.

The divine Master then begins with this sinner the sublime dialogue which the holy Gospel has transmitted to us. The respect of Jesus for souls, the rare prudence which accompanies all His words and all His acts, His sweetness, His patience, His humility are no less evident than His profound knowledge of the human heart. He first asks the Samaritan woman for a slight service. He endures, without any show of resentment, her impertinent remarks. He enters into her spirit, little by little, exciting her natural curiosity with holy skill. He thus leads her to declare the irregularity of her position. It is only when she says of her own accord: "I have no husband" (*John* 4:17), that Jesus lets her see that He knows the state of sin in which she has been living. But He does it simply, without making any reproaches to her, knowing well that she is not capable of receiving them; He does not chastise her for her contempt; He does not humiliate her by a single harsh word.

This admirable sweetness, this divine look which reads her soul, give this poor woman confidence to question Jesus. With incomparable goodness, He answers her questions, dispels her doubts, and enlightens her mind. When He has thus made Himself Master of her mind, He declares to her His divine mission. She, all excited, returns in haste to the town. A strange perturbation has taken possession of her soul; thoughts which she has never had before now trouble her conscience. Under the influence of grace, a change of which she is not yet conscious is being operated in her. When she returns to Sichar, she feels herself urged to tell everyone she meets: "Come and see a man who has told me all things whatsoever I have done. Is He not the Christ?" (*John* 4:29). She does not know yet whether she ought to believe; but she understands that this Man, so pure, so grave, so sweet, who has spoken to her by the wayside, is no common person. She wishes that others may form their own judgment of Him.

On the evening of that same night when Jesus, invited by the inhabitants, enters Sichar, He finds the sinful woman again; all-powerful grace has transformed her. She comes this time of her own accord to her charitable Saviour, not in order to avow crimes which He already knew, but to receive a pardon which her faith and contrition claim, and which the infinitely kind Heart of Jesus hastens to give her. Mercy once more triumphs; it has made from a miserable creature in whom everything appeared impure and vitiated, a soul enriched by grace, an apostle of truth, a glorious trophy for Christ. It has worked a new miracle.

And when two days later Jesus departed from the town, those whom He had drawn to His love, enlightened by His truth and saved by His mercy, unanimously gave Him for the first time this sweet name of Saviour. Already nineteen centuries have repeated this word of the happy Samaritans: "This indeed is the Saviour of the world." (*John* 4:42). Many other centuries will still repeat it: the echoes of eternity will repeat it without end! Yes, Jesus is the Saviour of the world, because He is Mercy: the world has such need of merciful pardons!

EIGHTH LECTURE

The Lunatic

*T*HE DIVINE Master went about thus doing good: from town to town, and from village to village, and while He poured out the treasures of His incomparably tender love, He often found Himself in the presence of a class of souls whose wretched state afflicted His Heart profoundly. The people, encouraged by these prodigies, brought to Him from all sides multitudes of sick and infirm, and in addition, poor creatures possessed by the devil, in order that He might deliver them. Doubtless, it might happen that several of these possessed people were not in the state of sin; the demon can, with the permission of God, possess bodies; but it is only by the disordered will of man that he can possess the soul.

Others, however, in great numbers, were groaning under the crushing yoke of double possession; that of both body and soul. What sorrow for Jesus when He saw the horrible disorders caused in the human soul by the spirit of evil! With what sweet pity He Himself came to their aid! With what eagerness He used His divine power to drive out the spirit of darkness!

At first, when we read the holy Gospel, it would seem to us that the only means used by Jesus to deliver these poor possessed ones were His sovereign authority and His all-powerful word. However, a passage of the Sacred Book tells us that He made use of other means also.

One day, the divine Master was descending from Thabor. He had just allowed a brilliant reflection of His divinity to appear to the enraptured gaze of His three privileged Apostles, and His beautiful countenance still retained the radiant imprint of the Transfiguration. It happened that a great multitude was assembled at the foot of the mountain; in the midst of this gathering, the disciples were engaged in eager discussion. All were greatly excited. When Jesus arrived, He enquired about the cause of the tumult. They replied to Him that a young man possessed by the devil had been presented to the disciples in order that they might perform the rite of exorcism over him, but that they had labored in vain to deliver him. The Saviour called the father of the unhappy one to Himself. He insisted on an act of faith and confidence before proceeding: then He had the demoniac brought to Him, spoke with authority to the evil spirit, delivered the poor possessed young man, and gave him back cured to his father.

The crowd having retired, and Jesus having entered into a neighboring house with His disciples, the latter, astonished at the failure of their efforts, asked Him to tell them the cause of it. The Master, always ready to instruct, revealed to them the insufficiency of their faith. He taught them not to rely in a human way on their own action, but to prepare themselves for the exercise of this divine power by confidence, humble, but assured and limitless, in the infinite goodness of God. Then He added: "This kind can go out by nothing but by prayer and fasting." (*Mark* 9:28).

How many lessons are contained in these few words! Then Jesus prayed, Jesus practiced austerities in order to save souls! The long prayers lasting through the whole night, the privations of every kind to which He willingly submitted Himself; the long journeys, the prolonged fasts, the lying on the bare ground—all these were the means that He used to deliver us from the yoke of Satan.

But had He need of those things, He, the Word of the Father by whom all things have been made? Would not a single word from His mouth, a single movement of His all-powerful will, be more than sufficient to expel the demons and send them back to the lowest depths of Hell? Without doubt; but let us not lose sight of the fact that Jesus has made Himself our Model. What He could do by His divine virtue, we sinners cannot do, even if we happen to possess a plenitude of divine gifts.

The most pure humanity of Jesus placed no obstacle to the action of His divinity, He could always act as God, He certainly had no need to have recourse to means other than His omnipotent will to accomplish His greatest works. Our human nature, stained by original sin, sullied by a great number of personal sins, or at least deprived of its primeval purity by the innumerable multitude of imperfections and weaknesses into which we fall each day, is a permanent obstacle to the operations of grace in our souls and to the full effusion of the gifts of God in us.

The priest is clothed by Jesus with His divine powers and, whatever he may be in himself, he is always a priest. From the day on which the sacred character of the priesthood has been imprinted on his soul, he has been able to do the works of the priesthood. He has entered into participation in the divine power in order to consecrate, to absolve, and to offer sacrifice. He may sin; he is still a priest—an unworthy priest, it is true, an object of horror for God and a scandal to the world. The sacred character shining on his forehead will only serve to light up the depths of his misery and the sad shipwreck of all his privileges; he is always a priest: "Tu es sacerdos in aeternum." (*Ps.* 109:4).

No doubt he can consecrate, absolve, offer sacrifice. But this divine communication of special graces for the priesthood, this power of love over souls to bring them to God, this authority over evil spirits to put them to flight, these admirable lights to discern the vocation of each soul, the designs of God over it, the way in which it must be guided, this courage to support the laborious works of the apostolate or to endure the rigors of persecutions, this eloquence to defend the truth, this strength to remain chaste, these privileges, these gifts, these graces destined by God for His priesthood, are given to him only in proportion to his love and his purity.

Now, to obtain, to preserve, to increase love and purity in himself, the priest must have recourse to prayer and penance. That is why Jesus said to His disciples: To drive out this kind of demon, in order to have a power similar to Mine, to do the works which I do, join to the great grace of the priesthood which I will communicate to you, and with which I have already clothed you in part—join, in addition, prayer and penance.

NINTH LECTURE

The Priest Pardoning with Jesus

*T*HE PRIEST, in the course of his labors for Jesus in the ministry, will meet with souls such as the Master Himself has encountered. Sometimes, he finds on his way poor creatures possessed by the evil spirit. What will he do for them? Will he endeavor to convince their minds? They are too far removed from him for his voice to reach them. Will he try to gain their hearts by his kindness and his devotedness? But they fly from his presence and reject his benefits. What will he then do in order to snatch them from Satan and bring them to God? He will prostrate himself in prayer; he will implore mercy; he will importune the Heart of Jesus; he will join works of penance to his supplications; he will renew in his flesh the sufferings of Christ, or at least he will impose on his senses that salutary yoke of the mortification which Jesus has constantly borne on His delicate body. Thus, uniting prayer and penance to the firmness of an enlightened faith and a boundless confidence, the priest will be enabled to drive the demon from the poor hearts that he possesses, and to destroy the nefarious influence that he exercises in the world.

At other times he will encounter souls like the Samaritan woman. It will be necessary to wait long for these and to act very prudently with regard to them. Poor souls steeped in sin! The priest will pray for them. He will be patient in waiting for them. He will seize eagerly every opportunity of doing them even a little good. In dealing with them, he will win their respect by his gentle and grave demeanor. He will convince them, not by violent discussions and heated controversies, but by language which is moderate, kind, simple, enlightening, but always humble. He will touch their hearts by a gentleness which has nothing of weakness, and by an interest in them which includes nothing of self. Like Jesus, he will never be astonished at evil; these expressions of astonishment are so hard on the poor sinner! He will never appear tired of listening to them or scandalized at their avowals. He will thus little by little succeed in revealing Christ, the merciful Saviour of souls.

If the priest meets with men like Zacheus, those souls, fundamentally good, but without light, souls completely immersed in worldly affairs, dissipated by the pleasures of the world, chilled by the intolerance of some pharisaically-minded Christians, let him go to them, let him treat with them with open heart, let him give them in his own life the example of really Christian virtues, let him show them Jesus in himself, Jesus with His Heart so good, His mind so broad, His virtue so simple; of their own accord, they will recognize the misery of their lives and the vanity of the goods for which they are laboring. Gained over by the meekness and the example of the priest, they will give themselves up to Jesus, the divine Priest.

And if the Master places in his path souls such as Magdalen, let him receive them piously from His hand. Let him purify them, let him instruct them, let him surround them with vigilant care. Let him cultivate them lovingly, in order that they may produce this exquisite fruit which Jesus expects from them. They are a divine gift which Jesus gives him, and he can love these souls, so pliable under his hand, so obedient to his voice. He may give them the best of himself, and cherish them more than others; but let this be always with the Heart of Christ.

Ah, this Heart of Christ, tender as the heart of a mother, ardent as the heart of a virgin, pure as the heart of a child, strong, generous and devoted as the heart of a father—it must beat in the breast of the priest! The priest participates in the power of Christ; he should also participate in His love. He is truly a priest only if he lives by the life of Jesus, if he acts by the virtue of Jesus, if he loves by the Heart of Jesus. Let him then attach himself to his divine Master; let him be inspired by His example; let him take counsel from Him in his doubts; let him get instructed by Him.

The mission of a priest with souls is difficult. It is a mission all of love and mercy. It requires great lights, much prudence, limitless self-sacrifice, untiring patience. Jesus Christ, God and Man, could worthily fill it, or those who, transformed by Him and living by Him, have with Him but one same heart and one same mind.

Jesus, we have said, is Love which pardons. Thus, although He cherishes the beautiful, pure souls who have always preserved the splendor of the divine resemblance, yet He has perhaps, an even more tender affection for those whom He has purified. "There is more joy in Heaven upon one sinner that doth penance, than upon the ninety-nine just who need not penance." (*Luke* 15:7). This Heaven is His Heart, His Heart the tabernacle of Infinite Love, from which joy overflows when He can perform in one soul His office of Saviour!

Jesus often wept over the sins of the world. He shed bitter and bloody tears over souls who, having strayed from the path of virtue, reject His mercy. How many times have we seen Him pour out His sorrow over faithless Jerusalem? How many times, prostrated before His Father, has He prolonged His prayer with tear-dimmed eyes to obtain for a soul the precious grace of repentance. At Gethsemani, not only did His eyes shed abundant tears, but His whole Body wept tears of blood. (*Luke* 22:44). The earth was bathed in this dew of love which Jesus poured drop by drop upon it in order to make it fertile. Yes! Jesus often wept over us.

The Gospel does not speak of His smile; He has however often smiled. He smiled at Mary, His Immaculate Mother, He smiled at the innocence of the children that were presented to Him in groups, He smiled at the disciples in the evenings after hard journeys, to encourage them and open their hearts. He smiled at suffering, as a beloved spouse, by whom He engendered the redeemed and the elect.

But the sweetest smile of Jesus was that which He reserved for His divine Father, the radiant expression of which no creature has ever been privileged to witness. When then did He allow this smile to appear? It was at evening time when He retired all alone to pray. If, during the day that had closed, He had poured out His pardons on souls, if He had untied the chains of many captives, then joy lit up His soul, and there under the vault of the heavens with its twinkling stars, before His heavenly Father who lovingly embraced Him, He smiled a smile of ecstasy in a transport of divine delight.

Prayer

O Jesus, Infinite Love, Merciful Goodness, Who hast come on earth to seek what was lost, to purify what was sullied, to raise up what was fallen, pour into the hearts of Thy priests the ardent zeal and the divine and tender love with which Thy adorable Heart has been inflamed. Grant that Thy priests, after Thy divine example, may give themselves with untiring courage to the search of the stray sheep, and that, filled with sentiments of piety and love, they may bind up their wounds and bring them back to Thy divine fold.

Grant Thy priests the grace to touch the hearts of men. Grant them the intimate consolation of gaining many souls for Thy love in order that they may one day hear from Thy mouth these divine words: "Come ye good and faithful servants, enter into the joy of your Lord." (*Matt.* 25:21).

CHAPTER IV

Jesus Consoling

SUFFERING was not created for man; it was to be the exclusive lot of the rebellious, fallen angels, who, severing themselves from eternal Love by an act, free indeed but an abuse of their free will, vowed themselves forever to eternal hatred. When man had sinned, when the divine plan formed by Infinite Love for His beloved creature had been upset and ruined, then suffering burst its banks and rushed upon humanity like a devastating torrent.

Man then began to suffer in every part of his being. He suffered in his body: work and its fatigue, the extremes of climate, troubles of sickness, accidents of fortune, all united to make him experience suffering. The marvellous structure of his body, the delicacy of its organs, the perfection of its senses which should have served to multiply his joys, after sin, served only to multiply his torments. There is not one of his members, in fact, not a fibre of his being but can sooner or later become sensitive to sorrow.

He suffers in his heart. That harmonious instrument, which should resound only under the delicate touches of the hand of God, sees itself tortured by the awkward hands of creatures. Its frail and melodious cords are broken in turn by the shock of ingratitude, hatred and abandonment, by the separations caused by death, by sorrowful deceptions and bitter disillusionment.

He suffers in his soul. Created after the image of God, the soul had been endowed with admirable faculties whose full and perfect exercise was to have brought him sublime enjoyment. But sin, by casting its shadow upon it and paralyzing the outbursts of its enthusiasm, gave entrance to sorrow. The intellect of man suffers from its powerlessness to know and penetrate mysteries of which it gets a glimpse. His memory suffers by the remembrance of past sorrows or lost joys. His will suffers from its revolts, its uncertainties, its variations. Man suffers in his imagination by apprehension about the future; in fine, he suffers in his whole being and at every period of his life.

In his cradle, he sheds tears, unconsciously, no doubt, but real tears, and he cries plaintively. His childhood, his youth, the years of his manhood have their sorrows and bereavements. His old age has its solitude, its infirmities and its regrets. Then there is death with its agonies and its anguishes and the last tears shed over the grave.

During the ages, that human sorrow has gone up towards Heaven like a cry calling for a Consoler, for man, when he suffers, has need of being consoled. He is too weak to carry alone the burden of his sorrow; he needs to be helped and sustained; he needs a hand to wipe away his tears and to bind up his wounds, an arm to raise him up, a voice to encourage and cheer him, a friendly heart to which he can reveal his trouble.

From the bosom of Infinite Love, an echo answers this suppliant appeal; the Word was made flesh! (*John* 1:14). Jesus, the divine Lamb, full of sweetness and tenderness, appeared on our desolate earth. He came not only to bring to ignorant man light and truth, to the sinner pardon for his crimes, but also to suffering and lonely man the heavenly balm of consolation. Who, better than the Word Incarnate, could fill the role of Consoler here below? Did He not know all the sorrows which He came to solace, and has He not sufficient love and sufficient power to be willing and able to give consolation?

He is God. He knows by His infinite intelligence all the sensitiveness of His creatures, and knows what trouble sin has brought to them. With the clearness of His divine eyes, He follows all their inward struggles and their most secret sorrows.

He is Man. He has experienced in Himself all the sufferings of humanity. On the days of His Passion, His Sacred Flesh bathed in the blood of the agony, torn by whips, pierced by the thorns and the nails, has suffered the most dolorous martyrdom. His Heart, overflowing with love, has been broken by ingratitude, jealousy, hatred and base abandonment. His soul has known the sadness of terror, unspeakable tortures and the anguish of death.

He knows our sorrows. Will He be willing to alleviate them? Just listen to these words of the Master: "Come to Me all you that labor and are burdened and I will refresh you." (*Matt.* 11:28). Come to Me, said Jesus, to Me, your Comforter! Come, ye suffering ones of this world, ye sorrowful, ye broken; all ye who, in your bodies, in your hearts, or in your souls, bear a bleeding wound to be healed!

And how will the adorable Master set about consoling us? Our sufferings are so numerous, our sorrows are so profound they seem sometimes irremediable! From His Heart, the sacred Tabernacle of Infinite Love, the flood of divine consolations will pour forth on the world.

In the course of His holy life, we shall see Jesus, tender as a mother, bend down over suffering humanity and pour into its heart an alleviating, healing balm. And when He has ascended into His glory, when He can no longer in His human form continue His mission of Consoler, He will not leave His own in abandonment; the Holy Spirit, the Spirit of Love, who proceeds from the Father and the Son, will be sent. He will exercise His consoling action in souls by Himself, through the knowledge of the eternal truths which He will diffuse in their intellects and by the supernatural unction of the Infinite Love which He will pour into their hearts. (*John* 16:7–14).

This consoling action will be manifested, especially by the Church, and in the Church by the priest. Behold the great gift which Jesus will make to His faithful during the course of the ages: the Church and the priest: the Church, truly Mother, always ready to wipe away man's tears, always ready to take in her arms and clasp to her breast those of her children that are pressed down by suffering; the priest, representative of Jesus, filled with the power of the Holy Spirit, bending down, like the Master, over all human sorrows, and pouring consolation into wounded hearts and bruised souls.

Jesus Consoling the People

*L*ET US NOW, with the aid of the Gospels, follow Jesus in His mission of Consoler, for, during the three years of His public life He does not rest content with purifying sinful souls by His sublime pardons (John ch. 4, 8; Luke ch. 7). He passes, as a most sweet Consoler in the midst of human miseries, healing suffering bodies, binding up the wounds of sorrowing hearts, pouring out into souls His peace, that peace which surpasseth all understanding and appeases all sorrow. (*Phil.* 4:7).

At the commencement of His ministry, He begins by transforming our ideas of sorrow. Before His coming, suffering had been a humiliation and sorrow a shame; a sick body was an object of horror; the groaning of broken hearts found no echo. But when on the Mountain, the powerful voice of the Master uttered that cry: "Blessed are the poor. . . . Blessed are they that mourn. . . . Blessed are they that suffer . . ." (*Matt.* 5:3–12), the human soul learned the value of suffering. Is it not a consolation to know the inestimable value of suffering, to know what it expiates, what it obtains, what it merits, to know the immense weight of glory that a few days of sufferings endured on earth will merit for all eternity? (*2 Cor.* 4:17). And what a supernatural and sublime consolation! It braces hearts for noble enterprises; it fortifies wills that are naturally weak in the face of sorrow; it multiplies courage tenfold by giving a glimpse of the immortal recompense.

In order to show us how estimable sorrow is, Jesus took it as His lot. (*Matt.* 11:28; *Is.* 53:4). He chose it in preference to all the joys of this earth here below. As we have seen, He subjected His human nature to the experience of all kinds of suffering to which our poor human nature is heir. He made Himself poor to console the poor; He consented to be rejected and humiliated in order to console those whom the world rejects and persecutes. He suffered voluntarily in His whole physical and moral Being (*Matt.* 5:3–12), in order that we might find Him near us in each of our sorrows.

His pity for the sick is profound. He cannot hear their complaints without His Sacred Heart being moved, and we see Him all eagerness to relieve them and heal their infirmities. It is in their favor that He is pleased to exercise His divine power. He drives no one away, however lowly or miserable or repulsive he may be. All those who have sick suffering from divers diseases bring them to Jesus. "But He, laying His hands on every one of them, healed them." (*Luke* 4:40). He goes tirelessly from place to place to those who have need of His help. And what sweetness in His words! With what delicate art does He not say the right word to those who press around Him!

With a heart full of compassion, He listens to the humble prayer of the officer from Capharnaum, who scarcely dares to entreat the Master for the cure of his sick son. In haste to give consolation to this father plunged in sorrow, He says to him simply: "Go thy way, thy son liveth." (*John* 4:50). To the man sick of the palsy brought to Him to be cured, who was brooding sorrowfully over a sinful past, He says: "Be of good heart, son, thy sins are forgiven thee." (*Matt.* 9:2). The cure of his body would not have sufficed to console him who was suffering also from the remembrance of his sins; it was necessary first to sooth the mental pain of the sufferer by granting him pardon.

One day in a crowd the Master by His divine knowledge perceived a great object of pity. A woman was endeavoring to approach Him, for she said to herself: "If I shall touch only His garment I shall be healed." (*Matt.* 9:21). Jesus filled with compassion, allowed divine virtue to go out from Him, and behold! the poor woman became aware that she was cured. Troubled at what she had dared to do, and still more so by the looks of those who surrounded her, she remained motionless and confused. But Jesus, in the excessive goodness of His Heart, found consoling words: "Be of good heart, daughter, thy faith hath made thee whole." (*Matt.* 9:22). It was faith that brought this woman into the midst of the crowd. The Master, who reads the hearts of all, knew it, and by these few words: "Thy faith hath made thee whole," He consoled her for the painful efforts which she has had to make in order to approach Him, and for the prolonged waiting that she endured in the hope of meeting her Saviour.

Another time Jesus visited the Probatic pool. Numerous sick people were gathered at this place, waiting for the miraculous movement of the water. Among them, the keen eye of the divine Consoler perceived a poor sick man with sad and dejected countenance. This man asked for nothing. He did not implore the Master to be cured, or ask for an alms. He did not know that Christ had the power to restore him to health. The Heart of Jesus guided Him towards this mute object of compassion and addressing the paralytic, He said to him: "Wilt thou be made whole!" (*John* 5:6). He, the divine Consoler, bent down over this afflicted one, over this man who has no one to aid or succor him, cured his malady and brought joy to his heart.

When the Master meets with hearts broken by the death of beloved ones, how He shares their sorrow, how He hastens to make use of His omnipotence to restore to them the objects of their affection! Jairus is plunged in despair. His only daughter is dying. She dies. His grief is so profound that he can scarcely believe that the Master is powerful enough to restore to him his child. He sends for Him however, and Jesus goes, for He is in haste to console this afflicted father. "Fear not," He says to him, full of sympathy: "Believe only and she shall be safe." (*Luke* 8:50). The child, restored to life, is given back to the grief-stricken parents.

But this does not suffice for the tender Heart of Jesus. He wishes that they may have the joy, not only of seeing their daughter alive, but also fully restored to health and strength. "And he bid them give her to eat" (*Luke* 8:55), and the Gospel adds: that "her parents were aston-ished." (*Ibid.* 56).

In the course of their journeys, the Master comes to the city of Naim. On entering the city He perceives a mother in mourning, following the lifeless body of her only son. Moved by this mother's sorrow, He pours consolation into her broken heart. "Weep not," He says to her, and the young man, brought back to life by the all-powerful word of the Master, is restored to his mother. (*Luke* 7:11–17).

Lazarus has just died. Jesus, who loved him as a faithful friend, is saddened by his death. He is saddened still more, perhaps, on account of Martha and Magdalen who, He knows, are overwhelmed by the weight of their sorrow. He feels Himself urged to go and console them. He takes the road towards Judea in spite of the prudent warnings of those who wish to dissuade Him from returning there.

Arrived at Bethany, He meets Martha and endeavors to console her troubled soul by reminding her of eternal life and of the eternal reunion. Magdalen in her turn receives supernatural consolations, but the converted sinner is in a state of mind that refuses all relief. Jesus trembles in face of such profound sorrow: He Himself weeps with the inconsolable sisters of Lazarus. (*John* 11:33–38). He goes to the sepulchre and turning to His heavenly Father, He prays Him to hear Him again: "Father! I give Thee thanks that Thou hast heard Me. I know that Thou hearest Me always, but because of the people who stand about have I said it; that they may believe that Thou hast sent Me" (*John* ibidem). After these words, He cries with a loud voice: "Lazarus come forth." And immediately this man who had been dead comes forth, his hands and feet bound with the grave-cloths and his head wrapped around with a napkin. "Loose him and let him go" (*John* 11:41–44), said the Saviour.

The priest, sent by Jesus, is, like Him, often called to console those who suffer from infirmity and sickness, to raise up hearts crushed by sorrowful separation. If he cannot, like His divine Master, cure and resuscitate the body, he can, by the grace of Christ who speaks by his mouth, bring comfort to many sorrows and dry many tears.

What a beautiful and consoling part of the ministry of a priest is the visiting of the sick! He ought to make it his sweetest recreation to go to these living images of the crucified Saviour, with all the tenderness of his heart. He can so easily lessen the intensity of their suffering by pointing out to them its value, and by directing their thoughts towards the hope of eternal happiness. Let the priest, then, use great prudence and most delicate charity in raising up those souls towards God, in order to make them understand the nothingness of the goods of this world and the illusion of vain friendships. When the body suffers, the soul is so easily brought near to God!

But in the consolations which he gives, let him be always supernatural, and let his words, like those of Jesus, be all full of confidence and hope. Faith in the divine promises, and confidence in the infinitely merciful love of Jesus Christ, that is what the priest should give, as the best and solidest of consolations, to those whom sickness keeps on the bed of pain and to those who weep by the coffins of their dear ones.

TWELFTH LECTURE

Jesus Consoling His Own

*I*T IS especially with His faithful disciples that Jesus shows His tenderness as Consoler.

One day, He sees them saddened both at the fewness of their number and at their poverty, and uneasy in face of the uncertain future which opened before them. He reassures them and raises up their courage, saying to them: "Fear not, little flock, for it has pleased your Father to give you a kingdom." (*Luke* 12:32).

To the crowds, the Master preaches truth in all its rigor: He announces to them the coming of the Son of Man on the last day, and the terrible signs that will accompany it. But for His disciples He has words of comfort; He does not wish to leave His own under such a painful impression: "When these things begin to come to pass, look up and lift up your heads, because your redemption is at hand." (*Luke* 21:28).

And when the three years of the apostolate of Jesus were nearing their end, when He is about to leave the world to return to His Father, His Heart is moved with compassion for His dear disciples, who were sorrowfully perturbed by the fear of His approaching departure. He seeks to console them by the sweetest of words: "Let not your heart be troubled," He says to them. "You believe in God, believe also in Me . . . I will not leave you orphans: I will come to you." (*John* 14:1, 18).

And Jesus then announces to them a new source of help. Faithful to those whom He has chosen, He will continue to live among them by His grace, to live among them by His Presence in the Blessed Eucharist; and, furthermore, the Holy Spirit will come upon them, He will fill them with light and strength and will complete their instruction: "But the Paraclete, the Holy Ghost, whom the Father will send in My Name, He will teach you all things, and bring all things to your mind, whatsoever I shall have said to you. . . . Let not your heart be troubled, nor let it be afraid." (*John* 14:26–27). "If you abide in Me, and My words abide in you, you shall ask whatever you will: and it shall be done unto you. . . . As the Father hath loved Me, I also have loved you." (*John*, 15:7, 9). "But when the Paraclete cometh, whom I will send you from the Father, the Spirit of truth who proceedeth from the Father, he shall give testimony of me." (*John* 15:26). "But I tell you the truth: it is expedient to you that I go; for if I go not, the Paraclete will not come to you; but if I go, I will send Him to you." (*John* 16:7).

During this last evening, the kind Heart of the Master pours the sweetest and most supernatural consolations into the hearts of His disciples. He has never shown Himself so tender, so confiding, so divinely familiar. It is because He sees that they are suffering. He feels their souls troubled by terrifying apprehensions, their hearts already bleeding from this separation, the hour for which was approaching and which was to be preceded by such sorrowful events. He knows well that suffering is good for those who are dear to Him, but like a loving mother, He wishes by the delicacy of His love to sweeten the sadness of His beloved disciples.

The dolorous Passion commences. Jesus is to drink to the dregs the bitter chalice. Far from thinking of Himself, He forgets Himself to console His own. Even when crushed under His heavy Cross on the sorrowful way, He still finds strength to uplift the courage of the pious women who have followed His steps. When hanging on the infamous gibbet, tortured by the most appalling sufferings, He still seeks to pour consolation into the bruised hearts of those who surround Him. To the penitent thief, He hastens to announce the joy that He has in store for him. Take courage, He seems to say to him, your suffering will not be prolonged. "This day thou shalt be with Me in Paradise." (*Luke* 23:43).

But it is for His Virgin Mother and St. John that His special consolation is reserved. He sees them plunged in the most profound sorrow, agonizing with Him and crushed at the thought of the separation! Is Mary to remain alone as one abandoned, without spouse and without Son, without defense and without support? How hard this abandonment would be, and how bitter this solitude! And John, John who has sacrificed to Christ all the affections of the earth, who has left all to attach himself to Him—is he going to remain without guide and without love? Must he deprive his young ardent heart of all human affection? No! Jesus finds for each of these two whom He loves a means to sweeten their sufferings; He gives them to each other. Mary will find another son in the person of John, and John will be able to give to Mary that all-pure and filial affection which he had for Jesus. Both will be united in the love of the Master; both will be consoled by recalling sweet memories of Him, by working to spread His doctrine, by making Him known and loved.

When Jesus withdrew from us His visible presence, He did not leave us orphans. He sent the Holy Ghost to the Church; and to continue His mission of Consoler, He formed the priest, this other self, whose heart He filled with all the tender qualities of His own.

What a beautiful mission is this mission of the priest! How sweet it is, but at the same time how difficult and delicate! To fulfill this mission in a worthy manner, he must know the sufferings of his brethren; let him endeavor to understand the inner sorrows which, as a result of sin, have invaded humanity, and which are sometimes all the more poignant and bitter because they are hidden deep down and concealed from view.

The soul and the heart of man are two instruments perfectly attuned to each other, but delicate and fragile. The hand which touches them must be light; it must however be a hand with decision, and without awkward hesitation. Whether it be question of anguish of the heart or torment of the soul, the priest-consoler must have perfect discernment. Souls are very different; the same trial, the same sorrow does not produce the same kind of suffering in each of them; for each soul, for each wound a different kind of consolation is needed.

A mere intellectual knowledge of human sorrows will not suffice for the priest to make him an efficacious consoler. The consolation must go to the suffering heart; it is from the compassionate heart that it must come. Let the priest, then, form his heart after that of His divine Master. Let him share in all the sentiments of tender compassion and supernatural devotedness of that divine Heart.

The priest-consoler must be, like Jesus, filled with goodness, patience and sweetness. The loftiness and purity of his sentiments will make him handle with infinite tact all the sorrows entrusted to him for consolation. Like Jesus, he will love to bend down over them. His mission is to dry tears, to bring back peace into troubled souls, and to pour supernatural joy into saddened and broken hearts.

We say supernatural joy, for the priest must be on his guard against ever giving human consolations. The truths which he preaches are divine truths; the word which he addresses to souls is the very word of God; the consolations which he pours forth should be consolations from the very Heart of Jesus, a Heart infinitely good and compassionate, but also sovereignly strong and supernatural.

The priest should strive above all to raise up souls, to make them victorious over trials, to prevent them from falling back on themselves. Sorrow is a salutary and fortifying bath which permeates and purifies souls; but human consolations and enervating words must not come in and destroy its beneficent action.

Jesus, in His admirable parable of the good Samaritan, seems to indicate to us the help, full of charity, sweet and strong at the same time, which the priest should give to the wounded souls that he meets with on his way. On the road from Jerusalem to Jericho a man is stretched out, stripped and wounded, his strength exhausted, and no help within sight. The travellers who pass by him and see him in this pitiable state remain indifferent, and go away without giving a look of pity or a word of consolation to this unfortunate man. A Samaritan comes in his turn, and his heart is moved with compassion. He immediately approaches the wounded man, binds up his wounds with care, and pours in oil and wine. Then, lifting him up in his arms with delicate precautions, he places him on his own beast and brings him to the neighboring inn. There, he lavishes care on him, and when obliged to go away on the following day, he entrusts him to the care of the innkeeper, and provides for his wants.

When the priest, whose office is to continue worthily the works of Jesus, meets with a case of sorrow on his way, let him not turn away. His heart is too good, too like that of his divine Master, not to be touched by the misfortune of his brethren. Consequently, he approaches, he bends down over this heart denied affection by all, over this soul wounded by the conflicts of life. He binds up these bleeding wounds with the bonds of tenderest charity; he pours into them oil and wine, the sweetness of his compassion, the strength of the great maxims of the Faith. By the ardor of his zeal, he raises up this weakened soul, and brings it gently to God. He introduces it gradually into those dwellings of divine Charity, where the heavenly Physician will Himself dress the wounds of His beloved creature.

Behold the work of the priest-consoler, a work of mercy and love: in him Jesus continues to live on, going about doing good, pouring out the treasures of His divine Heart, the superabundance of His soul penetrated with Infinite Love, on all those who groan and suffer! His intimate union with the Heart of the Master, his absolute dependence on the inspirations of the Holy Spirit, will make of the priest this perfect consoler that suffering humanity calls for, and that it needs in order to continue its mortal journey here below, without fainting on the way.

Prayer

O Holy Spirit, divine Consoler, sent by Christ to our desolate earth, fill the heart of Thy Church, the holy Priesthood, with the flames of Thine ardent charity. Humanity groans under the weight of Thy manifold sufferings; to continue its progress towards its eternal end amidst the shadows of sorrow, it has need of being guided, sustained, consoled.

O Spirit, substantial Love of the Father and the Son, pour out on Thy priests the abundance of Thy gifts. Pour into their hearts the sentiments of sweet compassion and of divine tenderness which filled the Heart of Jesus, in order that, enlightened by Thee, and penetrated with the charity of Christ, they may be able, by means of a renewal of faith and love, to give to the world consolation in every suffering and alleviation in every sorrow! Amen.

CHAPTER V

THIRTEENTH LECTURE

Jesus Offering Sacrifice

Figures of Sacrifice

G REAT SADNESS has spread itself over nature; man, the king of creation, who was to guide all other creatures to God, has himself turned away from the right path; he has offended his Creator and his God; he has sinned!

After the few moments of pleasure which follows his fall, guilty Adam is seized with fear. He knows the goodness of God, but he knows Him also to be just and powerful, and the thought of this power and of this divine Justice which is aroused against him, throws him into frantic terror. For the first time, man is afraid of God. When he hears the divine voice resounding in the Garden, that voice, so sweet and so grave, which up to then had been addressed to him only in paternal words, trembling with fear, he hides himself. (*Genesis* 3:8).

Soon the terrible sentence is delivered. (*Genesis* 3:9–20). Followed by his unfortunate companion, fallen Adam leaves the Paradise of delights, to begin on the earth, now become less fertile, and under a sky too often darkened, the life of labor, of struggle, of sorrow, which will be, to the End of Time, the lot of his posterity.

At times, however, memory recalls the joyous days of Eden, the days of intimacy with his Creator; he laments, he weeps. He seeks to find again the lost happiness, he seeks to approach God and to enter, as before, into communication with Him. But Heaven is closed to his gaze and deaf to his voice; in vain does man the sinner seek again to renew with his Creator those bonds of love which sin has broken. Being obliged to struggle against the unchained elements, against the forces of nature, now in rebellion against him, but which he had seen on the first days of his creation so submissive and so marvelously ordered, he feels more vividly the infinite power of God, His might and sovereign authority; and, penetrated with the feeling of his own weakness, and of his own nothingness, he prostrates himself in adoration.

When man realizes the infinite power and majesty of God, he becomes still more touched by His goodness. Almighty God might have annihilated him after his sin, or, if He willed to conserve him for long expiation, He might have destroyed that splendid beauty, those innumerable riches of the universe, which, though more difficult to reach, nevertheless, are still left within his grasp. Thus, in his misfortune, man recognizes the goodness of his Creator, and his heart is eager to send up to Heaven a hymn of thanksgiving and praise.

But then there intrude on this memory the last words which an angry God pronounced against him when driving him out of Eden. He sees again the flaming sword of the angel who guards the gate of the garden; and the remembrance of the terrifying manifestations of divine Justice arrests on his lips his song of thanksgiving and freezes him with terror. He trembles, he is confounded; he would wish to repair the offence at the price of his own life; but to the cry of desperation which he utters to Heaven, no response of pardon is given.

Gradually, however, calm is restored to the tortured soul of man. He remembers the promise of a Saviour, made by God, and kneeling down on the earth, so often watered by his sweat and his tears, guilty man endeavors, by his groans and by the vehement ardor of his prayers, to make the promised Mercy descend upon him.

Thus, almost at each hour, in his gloomy solitude and under the crushing weight of his sin, the soul of the first man struggles with and is torn by these different sentiments. And one day, urged by the desire to unite in one act and to present to God the intimate and personal expression of his adoration, of his thanksgiving, of his reparation, and of his suppliant prayers, he offers his first sacrifice.

Under the immeasurable depths of the mysterious azure sky, in the midst of this vast expanse of earth almost devoid of human beings, on a block of granite which serves him as an altar, man places his first offering. It is without value, doubtless; but he regards it as precious, because of the care and labor which it has cost him, and because he has discovered its utility. It consists of fruits snatched by the labor of his hands from the unfertile soil; of an animal which he has nourished

and brought up with care, the first fruits of his flock. He presents
this offering to God; he destroys it; he immolates it to the glory of
his sovereign Majesty, hoping thus to touch His heart and obtain His
divine pardon. And the Most High deigns to incline towards repentant
man.

We see, indeed, during the first days of the world, pious Abel offering his sacrifices to God "and the Lord had respect to Abel and to his
offerings." (*Gen.* 4:4). During the ages that followed, the Most High
continued to accept these sacrifices, and sometimes He even sent a
flaming fire from Heaven which consumed the holocaust (*3 Kgs.* 18:38),
the merciful reply to the feeble efforts made by man to approach his
Creator and his God.

But how can the Supreme Being, the Supreme Lord of the universe, accept such a sacrifice? How can the guilty offerer of sacrifice,
and the victim without intelligence glorify God, appease His justice
and obtain His gifts? God is Love! He saw sin covering the human
soul with its deformity, and long before man had thought of offering
sacrifice to Him, a sublime council was held in the bosom of Infinite
Love. The Word, the only Son of the Father, offered Himself to pay
the debt of guilty man. He would become incarnate in time, and Priest
and Victim simultaneously, He would immolate Himself voluntarily;
all glory would be restored to the divine Majesty: Justice would be satisfied by this reparation of infinite value; the sacred bonds, formed by the
love between the Creator and His creature and broken by sin, would be
renewed again forever in this divine sacrifice.

The heavenly Father and the Spirit of Love acquiesced in the pro-
posal of Uncreated Wisdom; Justice saw itself disarmed by Mercy;
Power and Goodness united to form a masterpiece: Jesus Christ, the
divine Priest and the divine Victim of the only Sacrifice worthy of the
supreme Majesty.

And that is how the imperfect sacrifices offered by man on earth
were agreeable to God; the most holy Trinity saw in them the figure, the symbol of the adorable sacrifice of the Word Incarnate which
would be offered up one day, and which by its divine efficacy would
bring about the definite reconciliation between Heaven and earth.

The human race at the dispersal carried everywhere the idea of sacrifice. Indeed, there is not a race, not a religion but has a sacrifice as the

basis of its worship. But man, by the perversion of his intelligence and his heart, was, little by little, to lose the knowledge of his God, and it was to wretched idols that he was to offer sacrifice almost everywhere. The chosen people alone, the holy nation called to preserve the worship of the true God, would continue to offer Him oblation up to the day when, that which was imperfect having given place to that which was perfect, the Priest of the New Covenant would offer to the divine Majesty the only Victim capable of pleasing Him.

Under the Old Testament nothing perfect and accomplished had ever appeared. The Levitical priesthood, like the soul of the Law, was weak and powerless. But another Priest, according to the order of Melchisedech, was to arise, Who sacrificing a Victim holy, pure and agreeable to God, would lead to perfect justice all those who were to be sanctified.

FOURTEENTH LECTURE

The Bloody Sacrifice

*T*HE TIME had come when the Law of grace was to abrogate the Law of fear. The long waiting of the patriarchs, the ardent sighs of the prophets, the groanings of the human soul had called down Mercy; the Word had become Incarnate.

Amidst the darkness of midnight, while in the heights of Heaven the angels sang the Gloria, the Priest of the New Covenant made His entry on earth in a lowly stable. The holy Victim whom He was to immolate had just been born. (*Luke* 2:6). The Victim, in a poor manger, is there stretched surrounded by brute beasts, awaiting the still distant hour of the great immolation. The Virgin Mary, the Immaculate Mother, taking in her hands the frail body of her Son, raised It towards Heaven and offered It to the heavenly Father.

Who will tell the infinite value of this first sacrifice, in which Jesus, on being born, offers Himself, in the plenitude of His Will, as the prelude to the great sacrifice of Calvary, and in which Mary, the Virgin priest, in a generous outburst of incomparable love, in spite of the rending of her maternal heart, offers in advance the fruit of her womb to the immolation of the Cross.

For thirty years, in the intimacy of their loving hearts, Son and Mother will renew at each instant this priceless oblation. On the day of the Circumcision, at the Presentation in the Temple, the sacrifice will be more solemn. During the years of exile in Egypt, in the calm and silent life of Nazareth, it will be continued; hidden from the eyes of men, it will not be less efficacious and sublime in the eyes of God. Jesus will remain during these long years, Priest and Victim; Priest, powerful Mediator between the Divinity and humanity; God and Man at the same time, and consequently alone worthy to approach God, to immolate to Him a Victim without stain, to offer to Him the sacrifice of adoration, praise and thanksgiving which is His due; alone worthy to intercede for His brethren, sinners, and to obtain by the ardor of His prayer, gifts from the Infinite Goodness—Holy Victim, always offered, the only one capable of being perfectly acceptable, the most sweet odor of whose sacrifice ascending to the throne of God, appeases His justice and obtains mercy.

The years will pass in this mysterious immolation. Gradually, Jesus, Priest and Victim, will arrive at the plenitude of age, and we shall see Him, in the Synagogue, and in the vestibule of the Temple, eclipsing, by the brilliancy of His infinite knowledge, the misused erudition and the pseudo-science of the Scribes, doctors and priests.

Soon, this magnificent temple raised to the glory of Jehovah and so marvelously constructed, will be destroyed and there will not remain a stone upon a stone. What matter! For the divine Priest, the splendid building of Solomon is an unworthy temple; for Him the universe is His temple; in every place and at every time He wishes to fulfill the functions of His Priesthood and to offer sacrifice. If He is a Priest, He is above all a sacrificial Priest, and the brazen altar on which holocausts were offered is not an altar worthy of the august Victim which the divine Priest is to offer.

This Victim is Jesus Christ Himself. Scarcely will He have left the seclusion of the hidden life, scarcely will He have been perceived by the Precursor, when the latter will cry out: "Behold the Lamb of God, behold Him who taketh away the sin of the world." (*John* 1:29). Jesus is the divine Lamb of the new Pasch, whose blood poured out will preserve from destruction those who shall be signed by it, whose bones shall be consumed by the fire of love, and whose flesh shall be eaten in a perpetual feast.

Thus, during the last years of His mortal life, Jesus will appear to us always and at the same time both Priest and Victim. He is Priest when we see Him prostrated in the Garden, or on the summit of the mountain, prolonging His prayer, with His hands raised to Heaven, interceding with His heavenly Father for fallen humanity. He is Priest in His zealous preaching, in His patient teaching, in the consolations which He pours out here below. He is Priest especially when He offers sacrifice, when, to the glory of His Father, and for the salvation of man, He immolates His sacred flesh by the manifold sufferings He endured up to the very hour of the sacrifice of the Cross.

He is Victim without ceasing: in His fasting and in His solitude for forty days, in the fatigues of His apostolic journeys, in the privations which He imposes on Himself, in the crushing sorrows of His Heart, in the bloody sweat in the Garden, in the tortures of His Soul, in the constantly renewed offering of His life, in the acceptance of His Passion.

Behold! the day of the great sacrifice has come. He, the supreme Pontiff, adorned in the purple of His own blood, His forehead encircled with the crown which the soldiers in the Pretorium have formed for Him, advances in the majesty of His royal Priesthood, followed by a procession of the people who slowly accompany Him up the slopes of Calvary. Arrived at the summit, the holy Priest stretches Himself on the altar, and the august Sacrifice is continued until the immolation is completed.

Jesus, suspended on the Cross, remains there Priest and Victim. Priest, because it is He who immolates Himself voluntarily in the full possession of His Will. Had He not replied to Pilate a few hours before: "Thou shouldst not have any power over Me, unless it were given to you from above"? (*John* 19:11). Will He not say in the midst of the indescribable sorrows of His death agony: Father, into Thy hands I commend my spirit." (*Luke* 23:46). And now does He not cry out in the last outburst of His sacerdotal soul: "It is consummated!" (*John* 19:30).

Victim! Ah, who can tell to what an extent He was so on the blood-stained gibbet? Who can count the wounds on His mangled body? Who can recount the torments which He endures from the rough-edged nails, from the horrible tension of the nerves, from the innumerable pains which tortured Him in every part of His Sacred Body, from the burning thirst which He suffered? And who can describe the martyrdom of His loving Heart at the sight of the tears and terrible affliction of His beloved Mother and His few faithful friends; at the sight of the ingratitude of those on whom He had lavished His blessings, of the contempt of the people who had acclaimed Him only a few days before, of the hatred of His executioners, thirsty for His Blood? And who will ever unveil the anguish of this most holy Soul of Jesus (in some mysterious way forgetting His divinity, and seeming to be abandoned by the Heavenly Father), which is agonizing in the night without help and without light: "My God, My God, why hast Thou forsaken Me?" (*Matt.* 27:46).

Yes, "It is consummated." Jesus Christ, Priest, has immolated Jesus Christ, Victim. Heaven and Earth are now reconciled. God has pardoned the iniquity of man. By this bloody sacrifice, Jesus Christ has rendered magnificent praise to Infinite Goodness by offering the greatest homage of adoration which It can receive. He has rendered thanks to the heavenly Father for all the gifts poured out in divine liberality on the entire creation. He has appeased divine Justice, which the sins of man had provoked and which demanded complete satisfaction. In fine, He has solicited and obtained all the favors, all the helps and all the pardons of which our poor human nature has need! All is consummated!

The Unbloody Sacrifice

*J*ESUS CHRIST, the divine Victim, has just expired; the world is redeemed, the great peace has been made between Heaven and earth. On the altar of the Cross, Justice and Mercy have embraced; and Infinite Love, overflowing through the Redemption over all humanity, restores to it the supernatural life that sin had robbed from it.

But if Jesus Christ has willed to offer Himself once to God, His Father, as a holocaust of love for the eternal salvation of His beloved creature, He has willed still more. Alas! in spite of the abundant grace of the Redemption, sin was to continue to be committed from generation to generation, so weak has human nature remained, and so audacious and provoking, the enemies that surround it. Man, too, was always to feel the inner need of approaching his God by the offering of sacrifice. That is why, the Priesthood of Christ not being extinguished by His death—for Christ remains a Priest for eternity—His sacrifice also was to be permanent; and man, weak and sinful, will always be able to render to God the worship of honor and praise which is due to Him, and will always be able to immolate the only victim which the Divinity will accept.

O incomprehensible mysteries of the power and wisdom and goodness of God! Was it not enough that the Incarnate Word be once offered in sacrifice? Must it be that the life which He has taken up again by His resurrection be immolated anew?

Let us leave Calvary where the body of the divine Martyr, inert and cold in death, stands out livid in the midst of the surrounding darkness. Let us bring ourselves back in thought to the evening on which Jesus and His disciples, gathered together in the Supper-room, were celebrating the ancient Pasch, thus adding the last link to the chain attaching the ancient worship and the Old Covenant to the New Covenant and the new worship.

It was the hour of the supper. Christ was about to be delivered up. Eager to leave to His Church—this beloved Church which He had just founded—a visible and perpetual sacrifice, His love invented the Eucharist. Christ, a Priest according to the order of Melchisedech, in the Majesty of His eternal Priesthood, offered to His eternal Father His Body and Blood under the appearance of bread and wine, and He presented them to His Apostles, whom He at the same time established as priests of the New Testament. "Do this for a commemoration of Me" (*Luke* 22:19), He said to His Apostles and their successors in the priesthood, thus commanding them to offer His sacred flesh and His divine blood in an unbloody Sacrifice.

This sacrifice was not only to represent the sacrifice of the Cross but was to apply its saving virtue to the remission of the sins that would be committed in the course of the ages. Had not the Lord said by His prophet that a clean oblation was to be offered in every place in His Name, which was to be great among the Gentiles? (*Malach* 1:10, 11). Thus in the Supper-room, in an instant, Infinite Love effected two marvellous creations: the Eucharist and the Priesthood.

The Eucharist! Jesus living in the reality of His adorable Flesh and His divine Blood, with His Heart so ardent and so pure, with His Soul so marvelously gifted, with His two natures united in one single Person! Jesus Christ, such as He was in His life on earth, such as He is in glory at the right hand of His heavenly Father, such as He will be for all eternity, whole and entire! Jesus Christ, God and man, the Word-made-man, in the sublime majesty of power, wisdom and goodness, in the incomparable splendor of His Divinity, in the profound humility, sweet gentleness, and merciful attractiveness of His Humanity! Jesus Christ!

Jesus Christ Victim, offered in voluntary oblation, not once, suspended on the Cross, but every day, at each instant, in the shade of the temple, in the depth of the tabernacle, in the ciborium where He elects to repose. Immolated, not once as on Calvary by unworthy executioners, while He utters a great cry to His Father, but daily throughout the whole world, by each of his priests, on an altar of sacrifice, in the silence of the holy species. Jesus Christ become the nourishment of man, the viaticum for his journey towards eternity, the sacred beverage which causes to germinate in the soul the flower of virginity, and the fruits of

the strong virtues! The Eucharist! all blessings, God, the unique blessing, and all the graces of redemption, of salvation, of eternal life!

O man! O privileged creature, rejoice! Your God is with you, He is
yours! He makes Himself your nourishment to purify you, to strengthen
you, to give you a share in His divine life! He gives Himself completely
to you, He sacrifices Himself for you! Humbly prostrate in gratitude,
adore the liberality of your God. The Blessed Eucharist is for you; for
you also is the priesthood by which the Blessed Eucharist is given to
you! Rejoice, O man; your Christ, your Priest, is eternally living with
you. You are going to find Him at your side in all the needs of your life.
If you are thirsty for truth, He will instruct you and pour light into your
intellect. If you have sinned, He is there to absolve you and raise you
up. If you are suffering, if the sorrows of earth press heavily on you, He
will console you. If you wish to find a mediator to approach the divine
Majesty in your name, to present in your name your sacrifices with the
assurance of being always favorably received, He will mount the steps
of the altar and speak for you.

The Christ-Priest, eternally living, lives in the priesthood. He
Himself is the Priest *par excellence,* the unique Priest of the Most High,
without whom there can be no priesthood. The priesthood of the Old
Law which had preceded Him, by faith in His promise and by the hope
of His coming, drew from Him in advance the efficacy of its prayers
and of its sacrifices. The priesthood of the New Law which Jesus Christ
has formed, issued from Himself and grafted in Himself, has neither
existence nor power but by Him. Jesus alone is Priest in the priests of
the New Law. By them He exercises His priesthood in time; with them
He will continue it eternally in glory.

If Jesus Christ lives in the Eucharist, if He lives in the Priesthood,
what close bonds should exist between the priest and the Eucharist! It
is Jesus Christ Himself who is this divine bond. But what ought to be
the fervent worship, the tender respect and love of the priest for Jesus
hidden in the Blessed Sacrament, who puts Himself in their hands,
and who thus make Himself Victim, doubtless for all the faithful, but
especially for His priests! In the Gospel, do we not hear Jesus during
the last Supper, when consecrating the chalice of His blood, say to His
Apostles: "This is the Chalice of My Blood which shall be shed for you
and for the multitude." (*Luke* 22:20; *Matt.* 26:28). Even at this solemn

moment, Jesus marks out His priest first; the rest of the faithful present themselves only afterwards to His thoughts.

Yes, it is first for them that He makes Himself a Sacrament in order to be their Companion on the road in search for souls, their faithful Friend and Consoler on the day of trial and the strengthening nourishment of their soul and body. It is by them that He wishes always to be offered up anew in sacrifice, by them He wishes to be given to all.

The Eucharist is the divine Treasure of the priest. Let him then guard it with vigilance, let him dispense it with liberality; for the more he draws from it to enrich his brethren, the more he will be enriched by it himself.

Jesus Christ is in the Blessed Eucharist: that is why the priest should have such ardent and tender devotion to this Sacrament of Love. Jesus Christ is in the priest. He is in him living and acting by His eternal Priesthood. What then ought to be the respect of the priest for himself? What ought to be his concern to make Jesus appear in himself in all his actions?

But, Jesus is, everywhere and always, Priest and Victim. The soul chosen by Christ to continue His priesthood participates in these divine offices, and is also, at the same time, priest and victim. The priest is priest to his God, offerer of the august Victim who alone obtains mercy; he is mediator between the divine Majesty and men, his brethren; he is a priest! We should see shining on his countenance the sweet majesty, the serene gravity, the assiduity in prayer, the gentleness and benignity of Christ-Priest. He is victim: we should see him humble and meek, always given and always giving, offered in perpetual sacrifice like Jesus Victim.

Offering sacrifice and being offered in sacrifice, such was the life of Jesus Christ; such ought to be that of the priest. But for you who have followed Me, said the Master, in My trials, in My joys, who have shared in My various roles, who have continued on earth My life of Victim and of Priest—"for you who have followed Me, in the regeneration, when the Son of man shall be seated on the seat of His majesty, you also shall sit on twelve thrones, and judging the twelve tribes of Israel." (*Matt.* 19:28).

Prayer

O Eternal Father, God Omnipotent, Thou Who hast loved us even to delivering Thine only Son to be at the same time our Priest and our Victim, our Mediator Who is always heard, and our superabundant ransom; cast, we beseech Thee, Thy looks of love on our altars on which the sublime Sacrifice is still offered.

Recognize in the priests who offer it to Thee the living images of Thine adorable Son. Like Him, they go about doing good, spreading the light, pouring out pardons, consoling afflicted hearts; they drink from the same chalice, they follow Him to Calvary and they become, with Him, holocausts of agreeable odor. United by the same priesthood to Thy divine Son, they are with Him the dispensers of Thine infinite charity and of Thy merciful love.

Grant, O heavenly Father, that the priests of Jesus Christ may, by Thy all-powerful grace, be rendered so comformable to their divine Exemplar that, on seeing them, Thou mayst be able to say: "Behold My beloved sons in whom I am well pleased: hear ye them." Amen.

✠ PART II ✠

The Sacerdotal Virtues of the Heart of Jesus

CHAPTER I

Jesus, the Divine Model of the Priest

*J*ESUS is the model on which every man ought to form himself. He is the mold in which the elect must be cast before being admitted to share the kingdom of God. But if He is the sublime type which every human soul ought to reproduce; if all men ought to regulate the beats of their hearts by those of the Heart of the Man-God, there are some more than others who should more particularly conform themselves to the divine Model.

These privileged ones called to follow the divine Master more closely; these happy beings who will live a life altogether like His, and who, by nourishing themselves on His Word and retracing His example, will be living images of the Redeemer—these are the priests of Jesus.

Jesus, the divine Priest, continues in His glory the works of His eternal priesthood, but He wishes that, throughout the ages, His "other selfs" pursue in the world His redemptory work.

Formerly, God had reserved the holy Tribe for His worship. He had taken it as His own; He had destined it for His service and had consecrated it. In like manner, in the law of grace and love, God has set apart for Himself a chosen tribe. He draws, from the multitude of Christians, souls more specially loved by Him. He renders them, more than the others, comformable to the image of His only Son. He favors them with more graces, enriches them with greater gifts, pours into them more love. He overwhelms them with divine privileges, and, clothing them with a part of His power, He makes them, by His holy unction, priests and kings, ministers of His justice and dispensers of His mercies.

The priest is another Christ; he is the anointed of the Lord. Marked by a sublime and ineffaceable character, he passes in the midst of men, towering above them with all the height of his divine dignity, and bending down mercifully even to their most abject miseries. He goes about among the people, as Jesus did, doing good, curing all infirmities, all weaknesses of the souls of men, pouring truth into intellects, consolations and pardons into hearts filled with sorrow and repentance.

He goes about like Jesus: in the world, but not of the world. He comes in contact with all sorts of contamination, but he remains pure; he walks in the midst of hatred, but he remains good. He passes on without looking behind him, without hoarding up any temporal goods for the future. Living all in the present, he pours out his soul by charity into the soul of the weakest and most miserable. He passes, yes, but his action remains. If his soul, his priestly soul, reproduces the Soul of Jesus Christ; if his heart, his priestly heart, is conformed to the Heart of Jesus Christ, it is no longer his own action, the action of a weak and limited creature: it is the action of Christ Jesus, the divine Priest.

The heart of St. Paul is the heart of Christ. Ah, if we could say always, "the heart of the priest is the heart of Jesus," what admirable fruit this priest of Christ would produce in souls! What miracles of grace would he not operate after the example of the great Apostle of the gentiles! But too often, alas! the grace of Ordination has not transformed the priest. His heart has remained cold, his soul has remained altogether human; his mind has not been raised above that of the ordinary man, and in place of being, by the splendor of his virtues and by the radiation of his sanctity, this brilliant lighthouse guiding vessels to port, lighting up the night and mastering the tempest, he is only a frail bark tossed about by human passions.

He has not gone up on a height from which he might have lighted up souls in danger of perishing; he has not been willing to remain on the rock from which he might have been able to hold out a hand to the shipwrecked ones of life. Had he done so, perhaps the foam of the waves might have sometimes dashed against his feet; the winds might have perhaps sometimes been unchained against him, but he would have remained unshaken, strong with the strength of God.

The priest should not indeed withdraw into solitude and hide himself in the shade of the temple. He must live among his brethren, in the midst of them, always ready, in an outburst of charity, to clasp in close embrace all miseries and all sorrows. He must be there, always given, and always giving, like Jesus, the wheat of love offered for the life of all. But if the priest must live among men, he must not live as a man. In order that his brethren may have confidence in him, in order that they may lean on him for support, they must see that he is superior to them, stronger than them, more enlightened, more pure, more detached, better, more truly holy.

It is by studying the Heart of his divine Model, by copying His virtues into his life, that the priest of Jesus will succeed in transforming his own heart. Let him go then to the divine Heart, let him penetrate into It by loving meditation; let him, above all, allow himself to be penetrated by the vital influence which escapes from It. Let him endeavor to think like his divine Master, to love like Him, to live like Him. By union, let him become one single priest with Christ, one heart with the Heart of Christ.

Jesus Christ, God and man, contains in Himself the plenitude of all gifts, of all virtues. But of all the perfections that are in Him, some may be more specially called perfections of His intellect; others perfections of His Heart; others still, perfections of His exterior. His divine knowledge and His wisdom are rather perfections of His mind, of His intellect; His charity and His mercy are, it seems, rather perfections of His Heart; His incomparable modesty, the attractions of His divine Person, are perfections of His exterior.

However, if we consider His Sacred Heart as the symbol, the organ or tabernacle of His Infinite Love, and if we think that this Love is the principle and the motive power of His acts, of His words, of His life as Saviour, we may no longer fear to call all that we admire in Him virtues, perfections of His Heart.

When Jesus calls His priests to His Heart, He calls them to the source of love; He invites them to come and draw from the fountains of divine Charity; but He wishes also by this to draw them to the study of His divine perfections. He wishes His priests, His beloved ones, to be like Himself; saints like Himself, good like Himself, truly formed after His own Heart.

Among the adorable virtues of the divine Heart, some are seen in particular as the sacerdotal virtues of Jesus. It is in His relations as Priest with His heavenly Father and with souls that He has practiced them; and He has even practiced several of them to serve as an example to those who, after Him, were to continue His work as priests and Apostles in the world.

Prayer

O Jesus, adorable Master, do Thou Thyself reveal to Thy priests Thine admirable virtues. They are adorable because they are divine; but because they are human also they can be imitated. Thou hast rendered them, by the strengthening influence of Thy grace, accessible to the weakness of man, and when Thou dost mark Thy elect with the sacred character which makes him with Thee a priest for eternity, Thou dost clothe him at the same time with light and strength.

Make to repose on Thy Heart those whom Thou dost wish to associate with Thee in Thy work; let them hear Its sacred beatings. Still more, make them enter into the intimacy of Thy Heart by holy contemplation. Let them draw the spirit of the priesthood from this source of love and truth: the spirit of prayer and devotedness, the spirit of zeal and meekness, the spirit of humility and purity, mercy and love. Amen.

CHAPTER II

The Spirit of Prayer, the First Sacerdotal Virtue of the Heart of Jesus

*T*HE MOMENT had come when Jesus was to manifest Himself to the world. He was going to commence His apostolic journeys, and go in search of the lost sheep of Israel. (*Matt.* 15:24).

Thirty years of hidden life, all passed in work, prayer and silence, were, it would seem, a more than sufficient preparation for His three years of public life. However, He did not judge it so, and we see Him, when on the point of entering on this new career, led by the Holy Spirit to the desert. He is going to make, in most profound solitude, in most austere penance, in most ardent and continuous prayer, a last immediate preparation. Doubtless, Jesus had no need to go to draw from the bosom of the Father graces and lights which He possessed in Himself by the union of His humanity with His divinity. But He wished to serve as an example for us, and to show His priests who were, after Him, to continue His work, both the sublimity of their mission and the necessity which they were under of seeking in God the lights, gifts and graces demanded by the formidable responsibility of their office.

Work for souls is the greatest work that can exist; it is the work of God. But how difficult it is! And how it should terrify a man who is aware of his weakness! When God calls one of His poor creatures to such a lofty mission, He pledges Himself at the same time to give him all that will be necessary for him. Nevertheless, if the heart of the priest does not put itself in communication with the Heart of God, if it does not go by prayer to draw from the divine treasures, it will remain empty, and will see itself in face of its great duties, alone with its own weakness and insufficiency. "Without Me, you can do nothing" (*John* 15:5), said Jesus. It is especially in the divine work for souls that the powerlessness of the creature is revealed.

It often happens that Almighty God sees that the will of the creature resists Him; then He either conquers opposition by the weight of the benefits which He bestows in His mercy, or He breaks the rebellious will. How can a mere mortal dominate this stubborn will and lead it on the narrow road of the Gospel? What can the word of a man do to shake rebellious wills, and what can the exterior action of a priest do, if the interior unction of grace is not there to make it produce fruit in souls?

Not only did Jesus pray in order to dispose Himself for the sacred functions of the priesthood, but, we read in the Gospel that, during the three years of His apostolate, He frequently had recourse to His divine Father. At one time, we see Him on the summit of the mountain spending the whole night in prayer (*Luke* 6:12); at another time, retiring from the crowds, He seeks a more favorable place for His prayer under the olive trees of the Garden (*Luke* 22:39), or in the peaceful house at Bethany. (*Matt.* 21:17). Along the roads of Judea or Galilee, we often see Him at a little distance from His disciples, recollected in prayer.

Every time that He is about to perform some great deed, or work some great miracle, He raises His soul by prayer towards His eternal Father. (*Luke* 6:20; *John* 11:41; 17:1). When He rejoins His disciples by walking on the waters of the lake, it is morning, and He has just passed a long night on the mountain all alone in prayer. (*Matt.* 14:23–25). When He wishes to open the eyes of the deaf-mute, He utters a profound sigh and raises His eyes to Heaven. (*Mark* 7:33, 34). By the sepulchre of Lazarus, after groaning in grief before the frightful spectacle of death and its corruption, Jesus raises His eyes towards His Father in a prayer full of love: "O Father I give Thee thanks that Thou hast heard Me. And I know that Thou hearest Me always, but because of the people who stand about have I said it; that they may believe that Thou hast sent Me." (*John* 11:41–42).

Very often the priest, in his ministry to souls, must walk over the abyss. He must also open the ears of the deaf and untie the tongues of the dumb; he must also raise up to grace souls that are sleeping in the corruption of sin. How will he be able to accomplish these divine works, if he does not go and seek in God the power which is wanting in himself? For these works which are so far beyond human means, the intervention of God is necessary.

After the last Supper, Jesus raises up His Soul in an ardent prayer. He prays for His Church, for all those whom His Father has given Him (*John* 17:6), and love overflows from His Heart. At that moment He fills the divine role of Priest, the role of intercessor between God and man, thus becoming a divine bond of union between the Father who is in Heaven and His children on earth.

Jesus prays for His own; He prays also for Himself. On His entry to the Garden of Olives on the night of His Passion, He feels Himself plunged in mortal sadness. Trouble takes possession of His Soul; fear and disgust seize and overwhelm Him, and from His broken Heart there escapes this dolorous cry: "My Father, if it be possible, let this chalice pass from Me!" (*Matt.* 26:39). But He prays and gradually calm is restored. "And there appeared an Angel from Heaven strengthening Him." (*Luke* 22:43). He rises, steeled for the struggle, ready for the combat.

In his sacerdotal life, the priest, separated from, and high above the ordinary life, has sometimes to struggle against himself; against the promptings of nature which, although purified and sanctified, is however not dead. When he returns to his lonely home, where he sees himself alone in an isolated presbytery, unknown, without earthly future, cut off from all human enjoyment, solitude sometimes weighs heavily on his human heart. If he feels himself invaded by sadness; if temptation, like the wind of a storm, arousing sleeping passions, causes inexplicable trouble in his soul, it is then he should have recourse to prayer. Like his adorable Master, he must prostrate himself before his heavenly Father. He must ask for help from on high, he must call upon this unique Consoler, this Brother, this Friend, this Jesus, who alone by His incomparable love can fill the void in his heart.

Jesus prayed on the Cross. While the mockeries and blasphemies went up to Him on the Cross, from His divine lips there descended this sublime prayer: "Father, forgive them, for they know not what they do!" (*Luke* 23:34). When darkness surrounded His gibbet and His Soul was tortured by incomprehensible abandonment, He uttered this cry of anguish, this piteous appeal to His Father: "My God, My God, why has Thou forsaken Me?" (*Matt.* 27:46; *Mark* 15:34). Finally, when all is consummated, it is a last prayer, a prayer of confidence and abandonment: "Father, into Thy hands I commend My spirit." (*Luke* 23:46).

Like his divine Master, the priest is exposed to mockery, insults and maledictions from the rough and ignorant crowd; let him pray for those who insult and mock him, and his prayer will cause graces of unhoped-for conversion to descend into their souls. Let him pray when he suffers; let him pray when he is in agony. Let the priest live by prayer after the example of his adorable Master. By prayer let him remain in communication with the Source of all blessings. The priest has much to give, let him go then and receive much from God.

CHAPTER III

EIGHTEENTH LECTURE

Devotedness, the Second Sacerdotal Virtue of the Heart of Jesus

O N ENTERING into the world, the Incarnate Word said to His divine Father: "Sacrifice and oblation Thou wouldst not, but a body Thou has fitted to Me . . ." (*Heb.* 10:5 et seq.; *Psalm* 39:7 et seq.). Yes, Jesus could have added: Thou hast given Me a body, a heart, a human soul; behold them, I offer them to Thee! I devote them to Thy glory; I devote them to the salvation of My brethren.

In fact, the whole life of Jesus on earth has been one uninterrupted act of self-sacrifice. He was entirely unmindful of Himself, and without reserving anything for Himself, He gave all He had. He gave His work and His repose, His time and His strength. He made a complete sacrifice of His own life, even before giving it entirely by the bloody sacrifice of Calvary. He consumed it little by little, by self-sacrifice exercised every moment. He gave His Heart to His brethren—that was the secret of this untiring devotedness—"He hath loved and hath delivered Himself up." (*Gal.* 2:20; *Eph.* 5:2). Jesus joined in His own Person the sovereign quality of Priest and Offerer to the quality of Victim. As Priest, He has not offered up in sacrifice any other victim but Himself, and it is by giving Himself and devoting Himself that He has been offered in sacrifice. But it was not a different priest and a different offerer that has offered Him and immolated Him; He immolated Himself. Truly, Jesus is at the same time Priest and Victim, the eternal Priest and the eternal Victim of an eternal sacrifice!

Jesus wishes those whom He calls to follow Him on the heights of the priesthood, His priests, to be altogether like Himself. The character by which He marks them, makes them sharers in the different phases of His own life. They are priests with Jesus Christ; with Jesus Victim, they are victims. They are called, rarely no doubt, to go with Jesus even to the limit of sacrifice, and actually to mingle their blood with the blood of the adorable Victim. However, a mystical immolation like the immolation of the Eucharist is demanded of them: and a visible immolation, that of self-sacrifice, is also demanded.

Jesus gave His labor and His repose. From the beginning of His public life, we see Him preaching from town to town, from hamlet to hamlet; teaching in the synagogues, curing the sick, consoling the afflicted. His days are not His own; they are at the disposal of all. He goes from one place to another, from one case of infirmity to another, from one sorrow to another, always ready to help, always good. His nights do not belong to Him either; those which He does not consecrate to adoration of His eternal Father, or to intercession for sinners, He employs in conference with His secret disciples. (*John* 3:2 et seq.). In truth, He gives all His time, all His strength also. Without regard for bodily weakness, He is always ready for work and loving services. How many nights passed without sleep, how many meals taken haste, how many days without repose! What fatigue in those long journeys under the blazing sun, what weariness in the midst of the crowds that press Him on every side! Nothing repels His devotedness, neither the calumnies by which His enemies seek to dishonor Him, nor the insults which they heap upon Him, nor the ingratitude of those on whom He lavished His benefits. He gives Himself, He exhausts Himself, He annihilates Himself by incomparable self-abnegation.

In like manner, the priest of Jesus should give himself to his brethren, to his eternal Father; he is not a priest for himself. When receiving the sacred character, he becomes, like Jesus and with Jesus, the possession of all; he becomes the holy victim offered to the Father for the sins of people. All that is his belongs to God, all that is in him is for souls: his work, his repose, his time, his strength, his very life no longer belong to himself; all is given, all belongs to God and souls.

This was well understood by the priest according to the Heart of

God who made this answer to those who blamed him for his excessive devotedness: "What is the use of a priest who does not exhaust himself?" What is the use of a cluster of grapes, if it remains entire, and if the grapes remain intact? If it is not drained of its juice, the wine will not fill the cup. What is the use of a priest if he has not, in a manner, exhausted himself?—otherwise God is deprived of His chalice, and souls have not their thirst slaked!

Jesus left all in sublime generosity. As the Word, He left the heights of Heaven, the ineffable repose which He enjoyed in the bosom of the Father, the radiant peace of the sojourn of eternal happiness. He left all that to take the form of a slave, to shut Himself up in the infirmities and weakness of mortal flesh. As man, He renounced the sweetness of home, the peaceful security of a life of labor and seclusion. He abandoned all to embrace a life of self-renunciation and sacrifice, full of uncertainty and anguish, of suffering and poverty. He did not seek His own glory; but allowing the glory to go back to His heavenly Father, He reserved for Himself nothing but suffering and humiliation.

In following Jesus, the Apostles, His first priests, abandoned all. Peter could truthfully say to his divine Master: "Behold we have left all to follow Thee, what therefore shall we have?" (*Matt.* 19:27). The priest must leave all, not that he is obliged to abandon everything literally, but his affections must be detached from all things earthly. This does not mean, however, that he must break the sacred bonds of family and friendship. Oh, no! Did Jesus love His Virgin Mother less because He gave Himself entirely to souls? Did He not cherish with special affection Martha and Magdalen and their brother Lazarus? Did He not allow John, the beloved disciple, to repose on His Heart? These sweet bonds which Jesus blesses are not of earth.

The bonds which the priest must break are the human bonds which hamper the impulse of his zeal. Let him deny himself (*Matt.* 16:24; *Luke* 9:22), his ambitions, his inclinations to repose, his natural views, his satisfactions that are purely human; all that belong to the carnal and worldly man, and all that is of earth; all that lowers and debases. Let him make for himself a heavenly family of souls to which he will devote himself entirely! Let him open his heart wide, let him fill it with the sentiments of the Heart of his divine Master! Let him give himself, let him renounce himself, let him forget himself! Let him deliver up his whole self with Jesus crucified! Let him be the bread of souls with Jesus in the Blessed Eucharist!

CHAPTER IV

NINETEENTH LECTURE

Zeal, the Third Sacerdotal Virtue of the Heart of Jesus

*T*HE ROYAL PROPHET, personifying Jesus Christ, thus exclaimed to God: "The zeal of Thy house has eaten me up." (*Ps.* 68:10; *John* 2:17). Zeal, this ardent jealousy for the glory of God and the salvation of souls, consumed, devoured the Heart of Jesus, and like all violent passions drove Him to untold excesses, to follies of love and devotedness. Passionately eager for the glory of His eternal Father, He resolved to oppose everything that might tend to lessen it, to break down everything that could be an obstacle to it. Being no less ardent for the happiness and salvation of man, He determined to combat unto death whatever might injure him and compromise his eternal happiness. This enlightened, burning zeal of Jesus always kept Him ready to fight against evil, always kept Him at war with the spirit of the world, of this world for which He refused to pray. It made Him condemn all that is false and unjust, all that is opposed to God.

Jesus fought against evil. Having come into the world to drive out the spirit of darkness, we see Him unceasingly engaged in combat with Satan. He drove him from the bodies of the possessed, He threatened him, He spoke to him with authority. He was not content with delivering bodies from him, He drove him from souls and pursued him under whatever form he hid himself. Jesus, the sovereign and infinite Good, found Himself in constant opposition to Satan, the spirit of evil.

Nothing stopped the zeal of Jesus. Without flattery for the great and powerful of this world, without desire to obtain popular favor, He attacked evil directly wherever He saw it. One day, He armed Himself with a lash, and scattered the beasts destined for sacrifice, and overturning the tables of the money-changers, He purged the temple of the rabble of traffickers. (*John* 2:14 et seq.). Jesus combated all errors. The adorable Master came to bring light to the world. He came to give it truth. All the errors which He met with on His road: errors of doctrine, errors of morals, all the false interpretations of Scripture, all the subtle evasions of the law, all the vain discussions on legal observances, all that was opposed to right reason illuminated by faith, were denounced by Jesus and mercilessly castigated by Him.

Finally, Jesus waged war against the spirit of the world: "Love not the world, nor the things which are in the world. For all that is in the world is the concupiscence of the flesh, the concupiscence of the eyes, and the pride of life, which is not of the Father, but is of the world." (*1 John* 2:15–16). It was thus that John, the beloved disciple, expressed himself, he who had reposed on the Bosom of the Master, and who, more than any other, ought to have known and understood the inner sentiments of the Heart of Jesus. All the words of Jesus, all His acts were directed against this spirit of the world, so opposed to the spirit of God. He assailed and broke down this wall of triple concupiscence which was holding the human soul prisoner.

The priest is the soldier of God. As formerly the legionaries were seen advancing across deserts and wild mountains, tracing out the roads of civilization; as they were seen fighting unto death for the glory of their Caesar, under the standard of the Roman eagles; so should the priest be seen constantly fighting for all that is good under the standard of the Cross, and struggling with invincible courage against the aggression of evil. He labors for the glory of his divine King; following Him, he marches to the conquest of the world. If he seeks to make himself master of souls, it is not in order to enslave them, but to set them free. Oh, how beautiful is the mission of the priest, how noble and grand! He is, with Jesus, the defender of truth; he ought to uphold His rights and make them prevail. By his word, if he has the gift of speaking; by his writings, if he can wield the pen; above all by his example, by his life, he ought to condemn all that is false, all that constitutes a danger to the treasure of truth, of which he is the depositary.

His zeal, ardent like that of his Master, enlightened by Faith, inflamed by love, ought to urge him to make all that is in him serve the glory of his God and the salvation of his brethren. The priest, created to sustain the divine rights, to defend the inheritance of Christ, to protect weak souls against the designs of their enemies; to extend the kingdom of Jesus Christ, and to procure His universal reign over minds and hearts, ought to steel his heart for the struggle. By his knowledge, by the purity of his doctrine, above all by his virtue; by the irresistible power of sanctity; by the tender and ardent zeal which love alone can inspire, he ought to be, like Jesus, and after Jesus, the light of the world, a light, brilliant, but also vivifying and warm, which will convince the intellect while inflaming the will, and which will take possession of the spiritual strength of souls and direct them towards the sovereign God.

How powerful that priest is who is filled with the zeal of the Sacred Heart of Jesus! He is the priest according to the Heart of God, ardent for the glory of the Master, passionately zealous for the salvation of souls, a real flame of love, issuing from divine Charity to inflame the world!

CHAPTER V

Meekness, the Fourth Sacerdotal Virtue of the Heart of Jesus

MEEKNESS is the outward expression of goodness, a delicate and exquisite form which makes it attractive. Goodness that is rude and badly polished is goodness without form, and will not be able to make an impression on hearts; but, when it is clothed with meekness, it acquires a sovereign power and attracts everything to itself like a powerful magnet. That was the goodness of Jesus.

Meekness, by tempering the ardent zeal of the Master, gave Him a sweetness and an affability which had the wonderful power of attracting souls. It had imprinted on His whole being such an irresistible charm, that the old, the sick, the infirm, went to Him in great crowds and followed Him wherever He went. "Learn of Me, because I am meek and humble of Heart" (*Matt.* 11:29), Jesus had said. This interior meekness penetrated even to His exterior and gained all hearts for Him. The people loved His conversation, they received His teaching, rendered simple to understand and so easy to embrace by the divine unction that poured from His lips. They followed Him even to the desert, forgetting the necessities of life, and when they had once caught a glimpse of, when they had once tasted the sweet charm of His company, they could not tear themselves away from Him.

"Suffer the little children, and forbid them not to come to Me" (*Matt.* 19:14), said He. Constantly surrounded by these frail creatures, He loved to take them in His arms, to bless them, to give them as an example of simplicity and purity to His disciples. He said: "He that shall scandalize one of these little ones that believe in Me, it were better for him that a millstone should be hanged around his neck, and that he should be drowned in the depth of the sea." (*Mark* 9:41; *Matt.* 18:6; *Luke* 17:2).

What benignity and what loving compassion for the sick and infirm who approach Him! How easily He allows Himself to be touched by the spectacle of their misery! He who was so thirsty for sufferings, so eager to shed His blood, so ardent for the cross, the thorns and the scourges, cannot endure the sight of the sufferings of His brethren. He cannot learn of infirmity without curing it; He cannot see Martha or Magdalen weeping, without shedding tears Himself. Thus, with what joy, and what prodigality He uses this power of curing and of resuscitating which He possesses in Himself, the divine principle of life and love!

He shows infinite patience with His disciples, still so carnal and so gross. He instructs them, He encourages them, He reproves them sometimes, but He does so with infinite meekness! After fatiguing labors, He invites them to rest: "Come," He says, "and rest a little." (*Mark* 6:31). When the thought of His death troubles them and makes them downcast, He seeks to comfort them in their sadness; He promises them a divine Consoler. (*John* 16:7). He assures them that He will be always with them. (*Matt.* 28:20). He permits John, the youngest and the most loving of the disciples, to rest his head on His Sacred Breast (*John* 13:23-25; 21:20), and to remain there like a loved child resting on the bosom of its father. Thomas sees Jesus replying to his resistance and incredulity by loving favors. "Put in thy finger hither, and see My hands . . . and be not faithless, but believing." (*John* 20:27). When Peter denies Him, He addresses no reproach to him; but to appease his sorrow, He gets him to make three acts of love, three protestations of devotedness and fidelity, which redeem his triple denial. (*John* 21:15).

All the words of Jesus breathe peace and goodness: "It is I, fear not" (*Luke* 24:36, et passim); "Be of good heart, son, thy sins are forgiven thee" (*Matt.* 9:2); "Why do you trouble this woman?" (Matt. 26:10); "Come to me all you who labor, and are burdened, and I will refresh you" (*Matt.* 11:28); "Peace be to you! My peace I give unto you." (*Luke* 24:36; *John* 14:27). The Prophet had said that His voice would not be heard uttering cries, and that He would not dispute in the public places. (*Matt.* 12:19; *Isaias* 42:2). Indeed, His words are full of meekness. His teachings usually take simple and gracious forms borrowed from beautiful, smiling nature around Him. And when His zeal urges Him to castigate the passions and crimes of evil men, we discover in His voice more love for sinners than contempt or anger.

If Jesus Christ displayed the exquisite meekness of His Heart during the time of His apostolate and of His risen life, it is above all at the hour of His Passion that He has given proofs of it. When at the end of the Last Supper, Jesus sends away Judas to his detestable work, He speaks so meekly that all the Apostles present think that He is sending him to distribute some alms. At Gethsemani, when the traitor-apostle approached Him and kissed Him, the Master kissed him in return and addressed him in these sweet words: "Friend, whereunto art thou come?" (*Matt.* 26:50). As soon as Peter had made use of his sword, He said to him: "Put up thy sword in to the scabbard" (*John* 17:11), and turning round to the wounded man, He healed him. (*Luke* 22:51). At the house of Annas, an insolent servant struck Him brutally on the face, and Jesus, receiving this cruel insult with incomparable meekness, said: "If I have spoken evil, give testimony of the evil; but if well, why strikest thou Me?" (*John* 18:23). Before the unjust judges who condemn Him; in the midst of the soldiers who treat Him outrageously and torture Him; before His people on whom He has lavished His benefits and who now insult Him and mock Him, He preserves unalterable meekness and remains as the gentle lamb in the hands of His executioners. (*Is.* 53:7; *Acts* 8:32). Not one complaint escapes from His lips while He is being nailed to the Cross, not a bitter word for those who crucify Him. (*Luke* 23:34).

The priest is called upon to reproduce in the world the meekness of Christ. He comes to conquer souls, and no weapons are more powerful to gain hearts than meekness and goodness. Let the priest of Jesus, then, make himself good with the goodness of the Saviour, full of patience and meekness, helpfulness and charity. Many objects of compassion will come to him, many weak souls will approach to find support from him. Souls languishing or wounded, hearts chilled by the unequal distribution of the good things of life, minds warped by the errors of the century, wills discouraged or led astray, will be directed towards him by the mysterious ways of Providence. Oh, how delicate and gentle his hand must be to bind up all these wounds! How sweet and patient his action upon souls! He can, doubtless, speak with strength, stigmatize vice, and warn sinners; but his words and the truths which he announces will be more penetrating and will have more persuasive power, if they are tempered with meekness.

The priest must make Jesus known, he must make Him loved by conveying to others, by means of what he is himself, what Jesus is, goodness incarnate. How often have not souls, on finding in the priest such patience, such meekness and such charitable help, said to themselves: "If the servant is so good what must the Master be?"

Meekness is a powerful magnet which attracts souls. It is the mysterious net which the priest, the fisher of men, will throw on the hearts of men to drag them from the abyss of sin, bring them into the barque of the Church and draw them on to virtue and the perfect life. The priest, faithful disciple, friend and companion of Jesus, most meek of heart, if he has modelled his heart on that of his divine Master, will be able to accomplish in the world the work of Christ. It is a work of love; it is the work of reconciliation, of peace and charity which the love, the goodness which is born of love, and the meekness which is the flower and perfume of goodness, alone can undertake and accomplish.

CHAPTER VI

Humility, the Fifth Sacerdotal Virtue of the Heart of Jesus

W HAT DO WE see in Jesus? Infinite greatness abasing itself; sovereign majesty descending; authority and limitless power bending down and making itself feeble. We see a God humbling Himself even to this flesh, heir to suffering and death. It is not, however, these divine humiliations of the Word which we wish to consider here; it is the abasements of His human nature. It is the adorable humility that He displayed during the days of His public life, which presents itself today for our meditation and especially for our imitation.

He commences His apostolic life by a humiliation: joining the crowd of sinners, He bows down under the hand of John the Baptist and receives the baptism of penance. In the desert, where the Spirit has led Him, He descends voluntarily even to the lowest depths of our misery (*Matt.* 4:1–12); He consents to be tempted! (*Heb.* 4:15). He allows the evil spirit to appeal to the natural instincts of His Humanity. He permits Satan to touch Him. Why this excess of humility, O my Saviour? It is that temptation is sometimes, aye, often a necessary humiliation for man. It makes him aware of his weakness; it puts him on his guard against the occasions of danger; it makes him turn his agitated and trembling heart towards Him who alone can sustain and save him.

For the priest, too, temptation is necessary. The priest is so great, his dignity is so high! Would he not be inclined to believe that the sacred character which he has received will make him exempt from the troubles of humanity? Would he not be puffed up by the divine privileges that have been conferred on him? And besides, what does a man know who has not been tempted? The priest, who is called on to instruct and to guide souls, should have experienced, if not all, at least a portion of their weaknesses.

When the divine Master expounds His doctrine, we see Him, it is true, sometimes sitting in the rich synagogues of Capharnaum or of Jericho; we hear His voice resound sometimes in the temple of Jerusalem under the splendid portico of Solomon; we hear Him now and then addressing Himself to the great ones among the priests, and to the brilliant courtiers of Herod. But how much oftener do we see Him surrounded by the people, speaking on the shore of the Lake to poor sinners, or satisfying with the miraculous bread the ragged plebeian crowd that follow Him to the desert. That is the charity of the Master. He wishes to save many souls, and He knows that the powerful and rich are the least numerous, and that the little and the poor form the multitude. That is why He goes to the little and the humble, because there, the harvest will be more abundant.

Oh, how far from the spirit of his divine Master would that priest be, who, disdaining the apostolate among the simple and the ignorant, would be willing to address himself only to the minds of the elite or of those on whom fortune smiles; who, finding that the poor churches of the country, or those of our populous suburbs, do not give sufficient scope for his talents, feels himself at ease only in the great pulpits of vast basilicas, and who would think the instruction of children and the visiting of the poor unworthy of his zeal! The priest of Jesus, on the contrary, entering into the thoughts of his adorable Model, sees nothing too low for himself. He knows the value of a soul, he knows that it has cost the blood of Christ; and to save a single soul he gives, without reckoning, both his time and his strength and his life. In order to give a little more glory to Jesus, he will willingly consent to be himself annihilated and forgotten.

The humility of Jesus appears also in the care which He takes to hide His action under the action of His divine Father, and as far as possible to make His own personality disappear. How many times do we not hear Him repeating such words as these: "I do nothing of Myself" (*John* 8:28); "And the things I have heard of Him, these same I speak to the world" (*John* 8:26); "My Father worketh until now, and I work"? (*John* 5:17). He seeks by all manner of means to veil the brilliancy of the great miracles which He works. To the blind that He has just healed, He says: "Take care that no one know it." He charges the leper whom He has cured that he should tell no man. (*Luke* 5:14). He expressly forbids the demons, who, by a mysterious compulsion, proclaim His divinity, to say that He is Christ the Son of God (*Mark* 1:23–25); and He calls Himself the Son of man.

But it is especially in His dependence, in this spirit of submission which He shows in all things, that Jesus manifests to us His profound humility. The first thirty years of His life can be summed up in these short words: "He was subject to them." (*Luke* 2:51). During the three last years He does not change His conduct. He shows Himself always and in all things dependent and submissive. Although equal to the Father by His Divinity, He does nothing, however, without having recourse to Him by prayer; He makes it His glory to do always the things that please Him. (*John* 8:29). He seems in a manner, to be oblivious of all His greatness, of all the gifts and privileges of His divine Nature and to remember only the powerlessness and the weakness of His human nature: "My Father," said He, in the Garden of Olives, "not My will, but Thine be done." (*Luke* 22:42). Jesus, the divine Legislator, shows Himself always perfectly obedient to the law of Moses, to its holy precepts and to the manifold observances of the Mosaic worship. He obeys not only the religious laws, but also the civil laws. He recommends the giving of the tribute. (*Matt.* 22:21). He pays the tribute for Himself and for His disciples. All legitimate authority receives the homage of His submission and His respect. He goes further; He willingly makes Himself the servant of all; of the crowds that surround Him, of those who at each step, stop Him to implore some favor. The centurion tells Him of the sickness of his servant: "I will come, "says He immediately, "and I will heal him." (*Matt.* 8:7). As soon as Jairus makes known to Him the death of his young child, He starts for the dwelling of the afflicted father (*Matt.* 9:18 et seq.): "The Son of man is not come to be ministered unto but to minister." (*Matt.* 20:28). His humility makes Him act as if He were under obligations to everyone.

Yes, even to his executioners, Jesus is obedient. He allows Himself to be stripped of His clothes, struck, clothed with the mock purple robe, crowned with thorns, He opens His hand to receive the reed that is placed in it as a sceptre. He carries His Cross, He stretches out His hands to facilitate the work of those who crucify Him. He presses to

His lips the sponge steeped in gall and vinegar which is presented for His thirst. (*Matt.* 27:34). When all is consummated, when He has, to the end, fulfilled the Scriptures and verified the divine oracles, He expires. Oh, how beautiful this submission of Jesus is! How touching is this dependence of the only Independent, of the Omnipotent, of the Sovereign Master! But what a lesson for man! Man, feeble and miserable creature, obliged by the condition of his nature to depend on so many other beings and on so many different things, is always seeking to free himself from this condition of submission, outside of which he can only fall into error.

Jesus, in a manner, turns aside from the consciousness of His Omnipotence, of His eternal wisdom, of His infallible knowledge, to consider in Himself only the nothingness of His state as a creature; but man, vain and proud, forgetting his inferiority and the trail of miseries which follow in his wake, loves to remember only what he judges to be his strong points, and all that can, according to his blind judgment, raise him in his own estimation and in that of his brethren. He always prefers his own manner of acting to that of others. The esteem which he has for his own thoughts, the reliance which he puts in himself, the confidence which he has in the certainty of his judgment and in the reliability of his mind, make him, in spite of his failures and meagre successes, disdain the counsel of the experienced, and the charitable warnings of the prudent.

Oh, how different is the priest of Jesus! Meek and humble of heart like his divine Master, he recognizes his weakness, he confesses his powerlessness, he distrusts his own views. He voluntarily bows down his intellect, the lights of his mind, and the aspirations of his zeal before the sovereign authority of God. And he sees the halo of divine authority shining on many brows.

A submissive child of holy Church, he sees in the supreme Chief the infallible representative of Jesus Christ. He loves to rely on the chair of Peter. The plenitude of the priesthood with which his Bishop is clothed inspires him with sovereign respect: he obeys him as the Successor of the Apostles, he venerates and cherishes him as a son does a father.

In the works which his zeal urges him to undertake, in the different charges entrusted to him, he has a humble distrust of himself. He is eager to seek light from those whom age, long sacerdotal career, exemplary life, or recognized virtue single out, and he is very far removed from acting by himself, or preferring his own counsel to that which he can receive.

He does not set a higher value on the works which he directs, or has accomplished, than on those which he sees flourishing with others. He does not desire to accomplish more, to succeed better in his enterprises, or to do greater things than those who, like himself, labor for the glory of God. This glory, the full expansion of the reign and of the love of God in souls, is all that he desires and is his whole ambition. For his own part, he forgets himself; provided that the good is being done, provided that his Master is more loved and better served, he is content, and rejoices as much at the happy success of others as at his own.

He willingly praises their talents and their works; he is edified by their virtues. If he sees any of his brethren stray away from the right path or fall into some error, he seeks to bring him back, if not by his advice at least by his example; he prays for him, he suffers for him, and he keeps himself always in a holy fear of falling into errors similar to those which he condemns.

The meek and humble priest who passes through the world is not only the priest of Jesus; he is the priest-Jesus. Yes, he is Jesus Himself, Jesus whose greatness is divinely abased by love, and whose sanctity has all the more brilliancy, whose virtue has all the more influence because of the mysterious shadows of humility which surround it. Humility has been, perhaps, the most attractive charm of the sacred humanity of Jesus. It gives a similar charm to the words and acts of a priest; it clothes him entirely with Jesus Christ.

Purity, the Sixth Sacerdotal Virtue of the Heart of Jesus

*N*O ONE has ever doubted the sovereign purity of Jesus. He was able to utter this challenge to the contemporaries of His earthly life: "Which of you shall convince Me of sin?" (*John* 8:46), without fear of being contradicted. His enemies, in their jealous fury, insulting Him to His face, called Him a demoniac and a blasphemer; they never dared to suspect His virtue. The multitude, in admiration of the great works of Jesus, and filled with respect for His pure and saintly life, recognized Him by the truth of His doctrine, by His justice and by the sanctity of His life, if not as the Messiah, at least, as a prophet, as the envoy of God. We, who know that He is our God, adore Him in His divine purity, which no stain, which no shadow has ever obscured.

He is the Pure One, the Saint *par excellence*. He, the Word of God, the Splendor of Light eternal, possesses in His divine Nature, brilliancy, transparency, luminous whiteness of which nothing created can aid us to form even an imperfect idea.

His human nature was perfectly pure, His Soul, on coming from the divine hands, had an ineffable splendor of innocence. His Heart, the tabernacle of Infinite Love, the sanctuary of the most adorable virtues, whose only throbs were for the glory of the Father and the salvation of men, was and always remains, the temple, the altar of the purest sacrifices, and the holy Victim consumed eternally by a sacred fire. His Body, formed by the Holy Spirit from the purest blood of the Immaculate Virgin whom the giving birth to her blessed fruit has rendered more virgin still; His sacred Flesh, which was to be immolated for sin and to become the antidote for this venom of impurity with which the blood of man had been inoculated by original sin—the Flesh of Jesus is more delicate, more pure, more ideally white than any idea that we can ever form of it.

Nothing can give us an idea of this adorable purity. The ray, issuing from the sun at the moment when it leaves its stellar source, when it has not yet passed through the clouds of the Heavens and the dense fogs of the earth—the ray issuing from the sun is less pure than Jesus! The white flake of snow descending from the icy regions of the air unsullied by earthly contact and poised by the winds in space—the white flake of snow is less pure than Jesus! The lily that has just opened out its petals in the depth of the solitary valley unsullied by any impure breath and untouched even by look, on whose petals no bee has yet come to rest—the perfumed lily of the valley is less pure than Jesus!

All that is in Jesus, all that emanates from Him breathes purity. The least of His words, the smallest of His gestures or of His acts, His whole Person, inspires purity, and diffuses it like a perfume. It is this that the mystic exile of Patmos seems to say to us, when, wishing to depict Jesus, He shows Him to us clothed in a long robe, girt with a girdle of gold. His head and hair are of dazzling whiteness, white like white wool, white like snow.

Yes, we do not question this exquisite purity of Jesus, and indeed it would seem superfluous to seek proofs of it in His words, in His actions, in the Gospel which makes it live before our eyes. Nevertheless, it is good for us, it is sovereignly salutary for our souls, to consider the esteem, the love of the Master for purity and the precautions which He deigned to take, not in order to preserve Himself, for He had nothing to fear, but to teach us by His example the prudence which should govern us in all our actions.

It is to the pure of heart that Jesus has promised the sight of God, this beatific vision which fills all our desires, which will satisfy all our needs. Does not purity of heart contain all other kinds of purity? If the heart is pure, the thoughts are elevated, the affections healthy, the words chaste, the gestures and manners modest.

Many a time during His public life will the Master speak of chastity to the crowd eager for instruction. But these divine traits of perfect chastity, this exquisite delicacy of virginity which the mass of the people, still too gross, cannot comprehend, He tells only to the ears of His dearest ones; He addresses them only to chosen souls who are able to fix their eyes on the towering peaks and luminous regions of the more perfect life. "He that can take, let him take it." (*Matt.* 19:12).

It is above all in the example of the Master that we shall find motives to urge us to seek out and love this angelic virtue. Jesus voluntarily embraced an austere and mortified life; He chose poverty with its privations, work with its sweat. He gives Himself to fasting, He imposes long vigils on Himself, He endures the incessant fatigues of the apostolic life. He sleeps on the bare ground, wrapped in His mantle. He gives to His body only what is indispensable, only what is necessary. Ah! it is because our divine Model knows that it is useful for us, poor children of Eve, to keep under the yoke and reduce to submission our nature so inclined to evil, and our senses so ready to revolt.

The Gospel shows us Jesus, it is true, taking part in feasts and wedding parties; but what does He do in the midst of those earthly rejoicings? Without losing sight of His great mission, He associates Himself with human joys only to bless them and sanctify them. Always grave, calm and dignified, He takes part in conversations only when He can, by His words, instruct, enlighten, edify and console.

A single word of the Sacred Book suffices to reveal to us the extreme reserve which Jesus used in His relations with women. Tired after His journey, the Master had seated Himself by the well of Jacob, and had begun with the Samaritan woman that sublime dialogue at the end of which the sinful woman became an apostle. His disciples returned to Him and the sacred text says: "They wondered that He talked with a woman." (*John* 4:27). They wondered! It must have been that it was very little the custom of the Master, a thing very strange and which the Apostles had never seen. However, we know that Jesus sometimes spoke to women. He spoke after her cure to the woman suffering from the issue of blood. He spoke to Magdalen to assure her of her pardon, to Martha to blame her for being too solicitous, to the wife of Zebedee whom blind maternal love brought to His feet to beg a favor for her sons. Yes, but He did not speak to them alone. It was in the midst of crowds, surrounded by His disciples, generally in presence of someone who could give testimony of the sanctity of His words and the purity of His acts. Even after His resurrection He keeps this reserve. He permits the holy women that He meets on the road to kiss His feet; but He forbids His beloved Magdalen, whom He sees alone in the garden, to touch Him: "Do not touch Me." (*John* 20:17).

When the prophet Eliseus sought to restore life to the dead child of his inconsolable hostess, he stretched himself over the little body. He placed his eyes over its eyes, his mouth over its mouth, his heart over its heart, he warmed it with his breath, and brought it to life again by contact of himself with it. When Jesus wishes to work His miracles, He avoids touching the body. Doubtless He wished thus to show the omnipotence of His word, He wishes also to warn us and put us on our guard against reprehensible familiarities and dangerous liberties.

Jesus is always careful to preach sovereign purity by His example. He wishes to see it shine in all His faithful. He traces its rules for all. But for His Apostles, for His privileged ones, for His other-selfs, what are not His divine demands!

You, priests of Jesus Christ, ministers of the most high God, dispensers of the divine mysteries, how great should be your purity! By your priesthood, God has placed you above the angels. He has communicated to you powers, He has granted you privileges which He has refused to these pure intelligences. You are called to render to the Eucharistic Body of Jesus the duties which the Immaculate Virgin rendered to the sacred Body of her divine Child. She held Him in her virginal hands; she wrapped Him in infants' clothing; she presented Him for adoration; she staunched His Blood running under the circumcision knife; she gave Him maternal kisses; she offered Him to His eternal Father and offered herself up in sacrifice with Him. Oh, how pure the hands of the priest ought to be that touch the sacred Body, that elevate It towards Heaven above the faithful prostrated in adoration! How pure those lips ought to be which each day give Him the chaste kiss of Holy Communion! How very pure those eyes ought to be that contemplate Him so often and so near under the veil of the Blessed Sacrament!

The priest should, if possible, be purer than the angels, and chaste like the Virgin Mother. But the priest is a man, and his flesh, like a heavy mantle, inclines him towards the earth and constrains him painfully. What then must he do to remain on the heights where grace wishes him to remain? He must walk in the footsteps of his Master, he must form his life after His example. If God has not given him the inestimable gift of suffering and sickness, he must supply for it by fatiguing his body by the laborious works of a ministry full of devotedness and sacrifice. He must embrace a life stripped of the satisfactions of the flesh and the senses, and he must endeavor to develop in himself the life of his soul and of his intellectual powers by study, by prayer, by constant search after the higher goods.

The priest is an offerer of sacrifice with Jesus, but he is also a victim. Victims ought to be pure, holy, and without stain, in order to be agreeable to God; a sullied victim is rejected by God; it is an abomination in His sight! Let the priest of Jesus, then, endeavor to purify himself still more from every human attachment, from every vulgar satisfaction, from all pleasures of the senses. He is not an ordinary man; he is a Christ, an anointed, a blessed one, a man separated from the multitude. He is so great, so worthy of respect and love when he appears in the midst of his brethren, pure, disengaged from grosser passions, elevated above all that is terrestrial and merely human! Can he who, each morning, quenches his thirst in the chalice of the altar, who drinks this sacred Wine which engenders virgins, quench his thirst with the pleasures of earth? Would he to whom Jesus offers the chaste intoxications of His love, endeavor to find elsewhere other delights? No, the priest will find, if he wishes, in the love of his God, in the Heart of Jesus, his adorable Friend, everything necessary to satisfy the legitimate needs of his heart and the aspirations of his soul, however tender and loving it may be.

CHAPTER VIII

Mercy, the Seventh Sacerdotal Virtue of the Heart of Jesus

*T*HE HEART of Jesus is the divine sanctuary where all the virtues reside. It possesses them all in an eminent degree. It is the sacred hearth whose fire is always burning and from which radiate all the moral beauties, all the gifts natural, supernatural and divine which our poor minds can imagine.

Among the virtues which dwell in the Sacred Heart as in their special temple, there is one, however, that seems to be more particularly His, His Virtue, His own inclination: it is mercy. Yes, mercy is truly *the* attribute of the Heart of Jesus. Holy Scripture, and especially the immortal songs of David, resound with the praises of the mercy of God, exalt it, and magnify it in a thousand ways. It was, however, only when Our Saviour had been given to us, that divine mercy appeared to us under a sensible form, palpable, so to speak, to the intellect of man and to his love. Under the law of fear, people got a glimpse of mercy; under the law of grace, it has been seen and touched.

Love was God; and Love was with God; and It has come into the world (*John* 1:1, 14); and when It covered Itself with the veil of humanity, when It descended upon the earth, It remained Love, but It took a new name and a new form. It took the name and the form of Mercy; It became Jesus or Mercy. Mercy or Jesus is the same adorable form of Love! All the words, all the acts, all the divine manifestations of this humanized Love, of this Jesus, bear the seal of mercy. It goes forth from Him quite naturally, as the water issues forth from its source, as heat escapes from the burning fire: "I will have mercy and not sacrifice" (*Matt.* 9:13) says He. His wish is to be merciful. "The Son of Man is come to seek and save that which was lost." (*Luke* 19:10). He has come to bring to the fallen creature grace of repentance and heavenly pardon. It is to save and not to judge that He has been sent into the world. (*John* 3:17). Thus, we hear Him say to His Apostles when they display too great eagerness in demanding justice: "You know not of what spirit you are!" (*Luke* 9:55).

This infinite mercy of the Heart of Jesus appears in a very touching manner in two incidents of the Gospel. Mary, the sinner of Magdala, repentant, and truly humble, comes into the house of the Pharisee to offer to Jesus the pious homage of her love and adoration. The Divine Master, who ordinarily rejects such testimonies, this time willingly accepts the tokens of her love; it is because He wishes to rehabilitate her publicly. And with what exquisite delicacy and with what divine tact does He not show to Simon how unjust was his opinion about her! Our Saviour loves repentant souls, and He declares of Magdalen: "Many sins are forgiven her, because she hath loved much." (*Luke* 7:47).

Another time, a woman caught in the act of sin was brought to Him. The Law ordered that such people be stoned. Does not Jesus always wish that people obey the law? Is not He Himself faithful to its prescriptions? What is He then going to do? Ah! fear not; His mercy will know how to suggest to Him a means to make mercy prevail over justice: "He that is without sin among you, let him first cast a stone at her." (*John* 8:7). All, one by one, have left the place. There remains no one but Jesus and the sinful woman. Great misery, and mercy greater still: "Hath no man condemned thee?" "No man, Lord." "Neither will I condemn thee. Go now, and sin no more." (*John* 8:10–11).

Nothing, however, is more capable of conveying to us an idea of the inexhaustible fund of the mercy of Jesus than these two adorable parables, real pearls of love, encased in the precious jewel-case of the Gospels; the Lost Sheep and the Prodigal Son. The merciful Heart of the Master, with its exquisite delicacy and its ideal tenderness, is so entirely revealed in these parables, that no human heart that is at all sincere can help being touched by them.

Jesus, the Divine Shepherd, has pursued His sheep. He brings her back to the fold. The fatigue and sufferings of the return are to be a just although very light expiation for her past faults, but the tender Pastor does not wish that she should suffer more. He does not wish that the return journey should tire her. If it must be that suffering and weariness are required to expiate the past, it will be He that will endure it. He takes the fugitive in His arms. (*Luke* 15:5 et seq.). He presses her to His Heart; He gives her privileges and caresses which she had not received in the days of her innocence.

And when the Prodigal Son returns to his father's home, what all-embracing pardon does not his father give him? Not only does he make him enter into all his rights for the future, but he wishes also that the bitterness of the past be forgotten in the joy of festivity and music.

Oh, how little is required to touch the Heart of Jesus and call forth His mercy! A word of confidence, an appeal from the poor thief crucified at His side, suffices to make Him pardon him immediately and open Heaven to him. (*Luke* 23:43). In truth, the spirit of Jesus, Jesus Himself, is mercy!

The great mission of the priest is to reveal divine mercy to souls. All have sinned to a greater or less degree. All feel that there exists between infinite Sanctity and their own miseries a chasm which appears to be impassable, and whose very sight terrifies them! There is in the depths of every human soul, even when filled with darkness, a vestige of truth which shows the Supreme Being to be infinitely holy and sovereignly pure. That is why, when it sees itself a criminal, it seeks to go away from God, it endeavors to forget Him, and being powerless to annihilate in fact this divine Being who will condemn it, it wishes at least to efface Him from its own memory and destroy Him in its thought. Then it always goes further into evil and descends into the abyss.

But when the merciful love of its God is shown to it, if it is even a little sincere, fear will disappear and repentance will take its place, and the grace of reconciliation will finish what mercy has begun.

It should be the priest's endeavor to make known Jesus under this most amiable, this sweetest and most attractive aspect; to cause the knowledge of His mercy to penetrate into souls; to open hearts to confidence and love. How consoling this mercy is! But what will the mere words of the priest avail to convince souls, if he does not show himself to be a true disciple of the divine Merciful One, all filled with sentiments of loving compassion for sinners? People must see him filled with a holy passion for the salvation of souls; they must see him following the footsteps of his Master, going in search of the lost sheep, without allowing himself to be discouraged by the length of the pursuit, or the roughness of the way. And when he finds these poor culpable souls covered with the shameful wounds of sin, let him take pity on them, let him bend over them, let him pour oil and wine into their wounds, and let him take them in his arms and bring them back to Jesus!

How happy the lot of the priest to be the minister of a God of mercy! His heart should melt in his breast by the ardor of inexpressible love, when he feels in himself the power of saying to the sinful soul these divine words: "I absolve thee!" God is never greater than in His divine pardons. The priest is never more elevated, he is never more clothed with God, never more truly Jesus, than when he pardons and absolves.

CHAPTER IX

TWENTY-FOURTH LECTURE

Love, the Eighth Sacerdotal Virtue of the Heart of Jesus

*T*HE HOLY SCRIPTURES teach us that the earthly Paradise was filled by the Creator with all kinds of delight. (*Gen.* 2:8). God had there His meeting-place with man and conversed with him in language ineffably sweet; and the charms of nature, so beautiful at the dawn of the world, served as a marvellous setting for these divine trysts. There, the sky was always benign, and the earth always fertile. The Tree of Life, growing in the middle, bore its fruit of immortality, and four streams, rising there and diverging, carried life and fertility afar. (*Genesis* 2:10).

May not the Heart of our adorable Jesus be compared with this Eden that was assigned as dwelling to the first representatives of our humanity? Is It not a garden of delights opened by God to souls urged on by an insatiable desire for light, truth and love? Filled with most excellent gifts, adorned with the most admirable beauties, true home of divine complacence, It is the meeting-place between God and man. The Divinity, lovingly abased, descends even to the misery of man; and man, weighed down by sin, finds there mysterious paths to ascend to God. In the centre, stands the tree of divine charity laden with the most exquisite fruit, and four streams of love water it and spread out, carrying the vivifying streams of sacred love to the world outside.

Infinite Love dwells in its plenitude in this adorable Heart, true Heart of the Word Incarnate. The Heart of Jesus feels all the ineffably pure and holy sentiments which the Divinity can. The Sacred Heart experiences all the noble and elevated sentiments which a human heart can experience. Its love embraces all worlds, no matter how immense, and all beings no matter how numerous, and submerges them in Its irresistible torrents; it is Infinite Love without bounds and without measure!

It seems to us, however, that in the Heart of Jesus-Priest, divine Offerer of Sacrifice, divine Victim sacrificed, love, directing itself to four different objects, has assumed four distinct forms: that it is divided, so to speak, into four currents of love, into four sacred streams with impetuous and fertilizing waves. Jesus loved His heavenly Father with the love of a Son and of a creature, full of respect and piety. He loved the Virgin, His Mother, with the love of a child, full of confidence and sweetness. He loved the Church, formed like a new Eve in His sacred side, with the love of a spouse, full of tenderness and fidelity. He loved and cherished souls, the innumerable multitude of souls, with the tender, foreseeing and devoted love of a father.

The Heart of Jesus has shown Itself to us as an abode of delights; is not the heart of the priest also the object of divine complacence? Is not this heart of man, so pure, raised so high above earthly corruption, so disengaged from human ties, also a spectacle of joy for the eyes of God? Doubtless, the heavenly Father takes pleasure in descending there when He sees it wholly resembling the Heart of His adorable Son. The priest's constant study should be to form his heart after that of his divine Model, to imprint on it the same virtues, the same purity, the same meekness, above all, the same love; is it not by love that hearts resemble each other?

The heart of a priest is a vessel in which God distills His heavenly love. This vessel ought to be very pure, it ought to be capacious. It should be vast as the ocean, and profound as an abyss, for the torrent of Infinite Love wishes to pass through in order to reach other souls.

The Heart of Jesus and the heart of the priest are a single heart with the same virtues, same grandeurs, same loving pulsations for God, for Mary, for the Church and for souls! "If any man thirst, let him come to Me and drink." (*John* 7:37). Let us go to this divine Heart, source of life and love; let us go to these fountains of the Saviour which are always brimming over; let us go to this sacred chalice which Infinite Love fills and let us drink to inebriation from it.

Love of the Heart of Jesus for His Father

Jesus loved His Father. One of His adorable sayings reveals to us His ardent and filial love: "I always do what is pleasing to my Father." (*John* 8:29). Is not the surest mark of love an inclination of the soul to do always what pleases the loved one, a loving attention to discover his desires, to embrace what he likes and to be pleasing to him in all things? The thoughts of Jesus have been always fixed on the will of His Father, the interior gaze of His Soul has been always turned towards Him. He took pleasure in the consideration of His perfections. He abased Himself, He made Himself little in order to exalt all the more the greatness of His heavenly Father. To repair His glory outraged by the sins of man, He offered Himself up in sacrifice; to extend and increase this glory, He spared nothing; He immolated Himself.

The dominant note of the whole life of Jesus was love for His heavenly Father. On the evening of the Last Supper, when but a few hours separated Him from His dolorous Passion, He sent forth from His Heart those sublime outbursts of love, adoration and filial confidence which we cannot read of without bending the knee and shedding tears. He loves His Father, and He knows that He is loved by Him; and this Infinite Love which goes from One to the Other in an ever-flowing stream has depth and ardor and purity and inexpressible transports: "Father, the hour is come! Glorify Thy Son, that Thy Son may glorify Thee. Now this is eternal life: That they may know Thee, the only true God . . . Just Father! the world has not known Thee; But I have known Thee . . . That all may be one, as Thou, Father, in Me, and I in Thee! That the world may believe that Thou hast sent Me." (*John*, Chap. 17, passim).

And when Jesus has accomplished everything, when He has to the end done the will of His Father, it is still towards this most loved Father that He turns to say with loving abandon: "Father into Thy hands I commend My Spirit." (*Luke* 23:46).

The love of God ought to be the dominant note of the life of the priest. Love for the heavenly Father who has made of him a creature blessed among all, who has marked him out from all eternity to participate in Christ's anointing; the love especially of Christ, of this adorable Master, of this incomparable Jesus who has endowed him with the most magnificent gifts, who has raised him to the highest dignities, who has made him His other Self. The love of Jesus, a love profound, intimate and living, ought to be the great motive power of all the actions, of all the thoughts, of the life of the priest. If he knows Jesus well, if he remains united to Him by love, he will work the works of his Master, he will have life in Him.

"He who loves Me, My Father will love him and We will come to him, and make Our abode with him." (*John* 14:21–23). This saying of Jesus is addressed to all the faithful, but still more to His priests. Jesus lives in the priest in a manner quite special: at the altar, in the sacred tribunal, in the pulpit of truth; it is not a mere man, it is Jesus, Jesus who teaches, Jesus who enlightens, Jesus who pardons and who absolves, Jesus who offers, and Jesus who immolates.

And when this divine Saviour has thus invested His priest, when He has filled him with Himself, when He has lived in Him in the three great actions of the priesthood, does He afterwards withdraw Himself? Most certainly, no. So long as a mere natural life, the disorders of the mind or of the senses, sin, do not drive Him away, Jesus continues to live in His priest. He lives in him to such a degree that He wishes the priest to say when speaking of His sacred Flesh and His adorable Blood: "This is My Body, this is My Blood." Oh, if the priest thought of this dwelling[5] of Jesus in his soul, of this sacred possessing, how he would love to retire within himself, to shut the door of the senses in order to converse at leisure with this divine Guest! Jesus lives in his soul. He lives there entirely, God and man, with His divine splendors and His human charms; with the power and wisdom of God, with the tenderness and sweetness of a brother, with the amiability of a friend.

---

5. Cf. Cardinal MacRory's commentary on previous verse:
    "In that day you shall know that I am in the Father, and you in Me, and I in you." (*John*, 14:20). "In that time, after I have come to you at Pentecost (together with the Holy Ghost), you shall know clearly that I am in the Father and *that you are in Me* as the branches are in the vine (See below 15:2) deriving all your spiritual life from Me, and I in you by *a special indwelling*, enjoyed only by the just.
    If there be a comparison here between *the mutual indwelling* of the Father and the Son on the one hand, *and that of Christ and the just on the other*, it is plain that the likeness is only imperfect and analogical. Yet such texts (see also *John* 6:58; 17:21, 23), even when we make all necessary allowance for the imperfection of the likeness, prove clearly how marvellously intimate and sacred is the union which exists between Christ and the souls of the just."
    See also *The Personality of Christ* by Abbot Vonier, especially Chapters XII and XVII.

The whole Christ lives in the priest; Christ and the priest become one; the divine Intellect of Christ is applied to the intellect of the priest and communicates to him Its light; the Heart of Christ beats in the heart of the priest and inflames it with ardent love for souls; the Body of Christ is united with the members of the priest, it imprints on them a supernatural life, and the grace of chastity. Thus, what reciprocal love should exist between these two beings! What exchange of thoughts, of sentiments! What union of will, what conformity of life, what harmony should exist between these two hearts! What intimacy between these two souls!

TWENTY-FIFTH LECTURE

Love of the Heart of Jesus for the Virgin, His Mother

JESUS loved His Virgin Mother. At the very beginning of His public life He wished to give proofs of His filial love. It was at Cana in Galilee. Jesus and His holy Mother were present at a wedding-feast, and, the wine having failed, the servants came and gave the news to Mary. Immediately, the Blessed Virgin turning to her divine Son said to Him: "They have no wine." (*John* 2:3). And Jesus answering His Mother: "Woman," said He to her: Woman *par excellence,* the unique, the only one among all, who is without sin, "What is it to Me and to thee? My hour is not yet come." (John 2:4). I have not yet commenced to work the great miracles which I am to accomplish. But by addressing yourself to Me in this circumstance, you wish, doubtless, to recall to Me what is common between us; you wish to remind Me of the sweet bonds which unite us, the community of life, of blood, of thought, of desire and of love which exists between us. Could I resist your prayer and not anticipate the hour which I had fixed? And the Mother of Jesus understanding His thoughts, sure of His filial Heart, turned towards the servants and said: "Whatever He shall say to you, do ye." And when the water pots had been filled to the brim with water, Jesus wrought His first miracle.

We are aware that these words of our Saviour have been given a different interpretation. But for one who had some knowledge of the Heart of Jesus, may not these words contain a delicate, affectionate allusion to that intimate union which nature forms between a mother and her child? Jesus wished that all should be in common between Himself and His chaste Mother. He associated her with His greatness, He united her to His joys, He made her share in His sorrows. He made her victim with Himself, priest with Himself, and in a certain sense, redemptrix with Him, the divine Redeemer. Love wills this union, this complete union of sentiments and operations.

The first look of Jesus as He uttered His first cry in the manger, was for Mary; the first miracle of His public life was wrought at her request, the last thoughts of Jesus on the Cross and His last look will still be for her. Seeing the Blessed Virgin standing at the foot of the Cross, agonizing in unspeakable sorrow, He leans towards her, and on the point of dying, He puts into her arms what was dearest to Him after herself: souls! It is His last legacy, it is His final gift of love. In the person of His beloved John, He has confided to her all His children. He has made her the fruitful Mother among all mothers, the Queen of the universe, the dispenser of His graces.

Among the sentiments of the heart of man, there is, perhaps, none more delicate, more profound than the love of a son for his mother. It is an exquisite mixture of strength and tenderness, of respectful submission, and child-like familiarity. When the son reposes his head on the bosom of the mother who nourished him, he thinks himself still little, still weak, but very much loved; when he presses his mother to his heart, he feels himself strong, ardent to defend her, powerful to protect her. With her, he is docile as a child, simple, and full of confidence. He speaks to her of his desires, he confesses to her his weakness, he tells her about his projects, he loves to take counsel from her, he would wish to obey her all his life.

Love for his mother is the first love that is awakened in the heart of man; it is also the last which remains. It is a love which guards, protects, purifies, consoles and sustains. It is a love, the only one, perhaps, to which one can give oneself with all one's heart, without fearing its being tarnished, without dreading bitter disillusionment.

For the man, for the priest, the mother is the gift of God. He finds in her, in her love so discreet, so devoted, all that his heart, especially if it be tender and ardent, can desire; he finds in her support, consolation, and protection.

If the priest ought to love his mother, if he loves her always, how much more ought he love the incomparable Mother, the Mother of fair love, his heavenly Mother Mary. We have repeated very often that the priest is another Jesus. What Mary was for Jesus, she is for the priest. She is a mother, she is a loving, helpful, devoted mother. She surrounds him with her care, she looks on him with love, she inspires him, she instructs him, she defends him, she blesses him.

What Jesus was for His Virgin Mother, the priest also should be for Mary; an obedient, respectful son, full of love. Let him always be with Mary as with his mother, a child. In his sorrows, let him hide himself in her arms, to her let him go in his joys, in his doubts, let him seek her counsel, let him have recourse to her in his smallest needs, to her let him confide all his desires and manifest all his weaknesses. Let him never speak nor act, nor even pause to think, without the ideally pure form of Virgin Mother of God throwing its protecting shade over him.

The love of Mary is a necessary element in the heart of a priest. It is the blessed ray of the sun, the beneficent dew, which causes the flower of chastity to open in his soul. It is a principle of life, a germ of virtue. The priest who loves Mary as a Mother, who confides in her, who depends on her, will not stray from the right path; he will remain humble, pure, fervent; in such a priest Jesus will live again.

The Love of the Heart of Jesus for His Holy Church

*T*HE love of Jesus for the holy Church is the love of a spouse. He left the delights of Heaven to attach Himself to her; He gave Himself to her entirely. He gave His Soul to her by applying to her, without measure or restriction, His divine intellect, His all-holy will, His memory and all the operations of His spirit. He gave her His Heart, vowing to her faithful, ardent, unique, eternal love. He gave her His Body, and in what an ineffable manner! He adorned her with the most precious jewels, He surrounded her with the most tender and vigilant care, He made her great, noble and honored, He rendered her fruitful, He adheres to her with inviolable fidelity.

What union has ever been more close, more indissoluble than the union of Jesus Christ with His Church? What love more ardent and strong, what devotedness more complete and thorough ever reigned between spouses? On the Cross, as on a nuptial bed, their mystical union was consummated. Since then, since these divine nuptials, they have belonged to each other forever. In prosperity and disgrace, in persecution and in honor, in joy and in anguish, they have never been separated. When Jesus has been despised, the Church has been despised; when Jesus has been abandoned, the Church, His spouse, has known abandonment; when Jesus has been praised and loved, the Church has been joyful. In like manner, all the outrages done to the Church have struck her divine Spouse; all the trials which she has had to undergo, she has shared with Him. They are so closely united and intertwined that the blows directed against Christ through the impiety of the time, have always wounded the Church, and some of the mud thrown at the mantle of the Church has always bespattered the robe of Christ!

The first tear of Jesus, shed in the manger, would have sufficed to redeem the world; less still, the first sigh from His Heart, on entering into life, would have been abundant ransom. Why then so many labors, so many sufferings, so many tears and so much blood shed? It is the love of Jesus for His Church! He wished to enrich her with divine treasures. He wished to clothe her in purple, and so He gave His Blood to dye her mantle; He wished to encircle her neck with precious pearls, and so He shed tears; He wished to crown her with honor and immortality, and so He gave His life and His honor to form her crown.

Can love go further? Can it stretch beyond the tomb? Can it survive death? When the husband has given his life for his spouse, what more can he give? Jesus has given more. He has taken up this life which He had sacrificed. He has transformed it, shutting Himself up with this new life in a narrow Tabernacle; He remains, for love of His Church, to the end of time, in a perpetual state of sacrifice.

And while He continues to immolate Himself for her every day, He continues to lavish His gifts upon her and to enlighten her with His heavenly lights; He warms her with the flames from His Heart, He nourishes her with precious nourishment, and this nourishment is His own Body, His own divine Flesh!

In the midst of the combats which she has to sustain—for her life is a warfare—He strengthens her, He furnishes her with weapons. In her anguish, He consoles her: He prepares for her, for the days of eternity, a definite triumph and a complete glorification.

If the Holy Church is the spouse of Christ, she is also the spouse of the priest: she is his chosen companion. At the hour when he was to give his heart and determine his life, he, the chosen one of Christ, considered in his soul to what side he would direct his destiny; and moved by the sweet impulse of divine grace and enlightened by the gentle beams which Infinite Love shed in his heart, he made a choice. Disdaining the beauty which passes, the joy which perishes, the fitful happiness which infatuates, and which death in the end always shatters; raising himself above the fleeting and deceitful pleasures of the senses and of the imagination, he has, by a free act, chosen the Church as his only spouse; he has taken her as his inheritance, and he has given himself completely to her. The sub-diaconate has been the day of his betrothal, the priesthood has been that of complete union. Now they walk together in life, they share the same fortunes, they suffer and they rejoice together; the honor of the one will be the honor of the other;

they can never more be separated.

Holy Church is so beautiful, with her youth ever renewed, defying the centuries which succeed each other interminably! She is so rich with heavenly treasures! Daughter of God, issue of divine blood, she is so noble and so great! With what love the priest should love her! With what jealousy he should preserve her in her integrity, with what holy ardor he should defend her against the enemies perpetually ranged against her! Indeed, she ought to be the great passion of the priest! To make her free and happy, to see her extend her influence from the centre of her splendid unity over the souls of the whole world, he ought to be ready to undertake all labors, to embrace all sacrifices.

The Church, with her dogmas so stable, her teachings so enlightening, her admirable hierarchy, with the marvels of virtue, of purity, of devotion which for the past twenty centuries she has produced, well deserves that the priest give himself to her with all the plenitude of his soul and all the enthusiasm of his heart. She knows so well how to give back what is given to her and give it back enhanced. She knows so well how to expand men's intellects, to elevate their minds and warm up their hearts again. When she takes a human creature, she knows so well how to transform him, perfect his faculties, enlarge his horizon, develop his power of being and of knowing. She is, with God, the great reformer of humanity; she is the wonderful transformer of souls, of societies, and of nations!

The priest ought to love this incomparable Spouse, as Jesus has loved her; love her in his works, in persecutions, love her even to the holy folly of sacrifice and the cross.

Love of the Heart of Jesus for Souls

W HAT SHALL we say of the love of Jesus for souls? This love has been His life, His raison d'etre. With His passionate desire for the glory of the Father, it has been the continual aspiration of His Soul, the beating of His Heart, the principle and the end of His actions, of His words, of all His thoughts. He was born for souls, He died for them, and in the thirty-three years which He passed on earth, from the crib to the sepulchre, this love, like a devouring fire, has never, for a single moment, ceased to consume His Soul.

Shall we quote some trait of the life of Jesus, some words from His mouth to convey an idea of the tenderness of His Heart for souls? But then it would be necessary to transcribe the whole Gospel! Is not this sacred book the poem of love? In its sublime pages, do we not see the divine Word, having descended voluntarily from the throne of His glory, exiled from Heaven, humiliated, degraded, hidden under the wretched garb of humanity, pass as a mendicant over the earth? Do we not see Him give Himself to the most painful labors, endure the greatest sufferings, and finally offer Himself to death? And all this to conquer the human soul, to unite Himself to it in an embrace of love!

If we approach the Cross, if we detach from its branches the empurpled fruit suspended there, if we press this divine fruit ripened in the sun of sorrow, love flows from it in streams. It is nothing but love. It is impossible to contemplate Jesus Christ on the Cross without being persuaded of His infinite love for souls.

Has He not said: "Greater love than this no man hath, that a man lay down his life for his friends"? (*John* 15:13).

What wonderful love He had for souls! In the first place He gave His life drop by drop by constant prayer, by long labors, by three years of apostolic journeys, of sermons, of privations, of circumstances which were tests of courage; by the constant weight of sorrow laid upon His Soul by the multitude of the sins of men. In fine, He yielded up His pure and holy life by the total effusion of His Blood, begun in the Garden of Olives in the prostration of the Agony, continued in the Pretorium under the whips of the scourging and the thorns of the crown, completed on Calvary by the nails of the crucifixion, and finished by the thrust of the lance which opened His side.

If we cannot look on the Cross without believing in love, we cannot approach the tabernacle without feeling ourselves immersed in its living waves. Love inevitably tends to union. The desire to unite Himself to souls has been continual and pressing in the Heart of Jesus. This need of union, it would seem, has been the great torment of the Master, and, to satisfy it, He has invented means altogether new. He has surmounted all obstacles, He has displayed all His power as God.

After uniting Himself to man by conformity of nature, He has made this union with Himself closer by a perfect resemblance of life, of labors, of sentiments and roles. He has wished to dwell in the human soul by His grace; but this union does not yet suffice for Him. He has found in His wisdom, and by His power He has operated an intimate, real union, up to then unheard of; a union by which He comes to live in us spiritually, in which He vivifies by His divine influence all the parts of our being; the Eucharistic union!

Behold the masterpiece of love! More loving and devoted than a father who nourishes his children by the fruit of his labor, more tender than a mother who gives them her milk, Jesus makes Himself bread, to nourish His beloved creatures with Himself. He penetrates into us, and penetrates us with Himself. By His divine Substance, He vivifies our substance. He incorporates Himself with us, He becomes one with us and we become one with Him! Oh, ineffable love of Jesus for our souls! For them, for each of them, He sacrifices Himself and gives Himself, He exhausts Himself and annihilates Himself!

Love for souls reigns in the heart of the priest, as in the Heart of Jesus, for these two hearts, united in the same loves, henceforth form but one. Before all, the priest loves souls because his Master has loved them. He is willing to sacrifice himself for them because Jesus offered Himself in sacrifice for their salvation. The need which he has to imitate his adorable Model in everything urges him with irresistible force towards these souls, so ardently loved by Jesus.

Other motives also urge him to cherish them: he has been created by Love, he has been created for souls. God is Love: all that goes out from Him is Love, all the beings which He has created are creations of love. But most particularly the priest is a creation of love. God has so loved souls, that He gives them His only Son; the Word has so loved them, that He became incarnate and offered Himself up in sacrifice for them! And when Jesus, in obedience to the will of His Father, ascended to His glory, God, in His love, created the priest for souls, in order that there might be always other Jesus Christs with them, to instruct them, console them, absolve them and love them.

The reason why the priest should love souls so much is that he is what he is, the privileged one of God, another Jesus, only for them, and on account of them. The priest has been given to souls and souls are given to the priest. From this double donation there should result in the heart of the priest a devotedness, a zeal, a tenderness which approach the infinite. It is the creature of God that he loves in souls; the object of the passionate love of his Master, the special gift of divine love. Souls are the raison d'etre of the graces, the favors and the privileges which have been granted to him; they are the cause of his greatness!

Souls belong to God, and the priest belongs to souls. To them, then, belong his labors, his sweat, his tears and his blood. To them belong the labors of his intellect, the determination of his will; to them belong his words, his thoughts, the activity of his life; to them belong the first bursts of the enthusiasm of his youth, the virile works of his manhood, the last works and the last efforts of his old age.

Jesus has loved souls, and He has proved His love by suffering for them and by uniting Himself to them even to making Himself their nourishment. The priest of Jesus follows the example of his divine Master, he enters into His loving dispositions, he shares His sentiments. He suffers for souls, and sometimes very painfully, but in the anguish of spiritual childbirth, he rejoices, for he knows that it is by suffering thus he gives new children to God. He unites himself to them by giving himself entirely, by living only for them, by making everything in him serve for their good, for their salvation.

This eternal salvation of souls is the great, the only thought of the priest; the conquest of a single one more to the love of Jesus is his greatest joy. With his eyes fixed on God, he goes ever forward in his sublime conquests. This holy passion for souls dominates him to such a point that he forgets himself completely. His happiness, his sovereign consolation, is to be able to lay at the feet of his adorable Master the fruit of his labors, the love-trophies of his pacific victories. To open the bosom of Mercy to a sinner; to wash away from these images of God the defilement which sullies them, and by incessant toil, by successive touches to remake the divine resemblance; to see masterpieces of sanctity being formed under his hands—these are the sacred joys, this is the divine intoxication which love for souls has in store for the priest of Jesus!

Bossuet says somewhere, when speaking of the Blessed Virgin: "Mary is Christ commenced." The priest is Christ continued. His life is, as it were, a prolongation of the earthly life of Jesus across the centuries. His word is not an echo more or less sonorous of the word of the Master; it is the very word of Jesus ringing through the voice of the priest, for has not our divine Saviour said to His priests: "He that heareth you heareth Me"? (*Luke* 10:16).

If such be the case, if the priest is another Christ, with what respect should he not be surrounded? He still finds this respect, this honor due to his character in those who have kept a right conscience and an appreciation of great things. But he often suffers insults, and it is for him an honor and a joy to be in that conformable to his divine Master.

But does the priest always respect himself sufficiently? Has he an adequate idea of his dignity, and of his greatness? Does he know what adoration and thanksgiving he owes to God, what love and intimacy he owes to Jesus Christ, and what edification and devotedness he owes to his brethren? It is the ardent desire of Jesus Christ to see his priests, penetrated with the sublimity of their character, and, at the same time, with the consciousness of their own weakness, come to His Sacred Heart and receive from that divine furnace both the light which illuminates and the warmth which vivifies.

Go then, priest of Jesus, to the fountains of the Saviour. Go and press your lips to this wound of love, this living fountain from which the Blood of your chalices issues forth. Go to this hearth of Infinite Love, fill your hearts, fill your breasts with its fire, fill yourselves with love and diffuse it all over the world. Jesus has brought fire on the earth;

His desire is that it be enkindled and that it burn (*Luke* 12:49), and it is for you, priests of Jesus Christ, to fan these divine flames and to inflame the world with love.

✠ PART III ✠

The Love of the Word Incarnate for Priests

CHAPTER I

TWENTY-EIGHTH LECTURE

Love of Jesus for His Priests before His Birth

*T*HE DIVINE WORD, God of God, Light of Light, begotten and not created, begotten by Infinite Love, Love Itself, thus truly Love which is truly God, has remained what He is in the Incarnation. And because Jesus Christ, the Word Incarnate, is God, He is also Love.

The most sacred Humanity of Jesus, united to this Love, penetrated by It, loved by It, must love and does love; it loves passionately, ardently. It loves during the whole course of His life on earth with a plenitude, an ardor which nothing can equal. His Heart has throbs of love which our hearts have never felt.

Now that the Saviour is in His glory, He continues to love. He will love during the immense space of time without end, and as Jesus risen from the dead dies no more, His Heart therefore can never cease to love. It will love for all eternity with a love without diminution, without end!

This love of the Sacred Heart of Jesus, which will never have an end, had however a beginning. The Word has always loved; but the human Heart of Jesus, formed in time, did begin to beat one day; one day It began to love.

When we see a great river roll its beautiful waters majestically forward, we quite naturally think that these waters which push each other on and follow each other, will go at last and lose themselves in the vast sea, in that immense ocean with which they will mingle. But sometimes our thoughts are carried towards the source from which this stream with its great waves, has come forth, and we love to go up its course and search for the place, usually solitary and hidden, from which the first drops of its waters gush forth. Thus, meditating on the

111

Infinite Love of the Heart of Jesus, we not only love to consider it in its eternal duration; we also find a most sweet enjoyment in seeking the beginning of this love, and going back to the first beats of this Sacred Heart.

The Word descended at the Incarnation to repair the glory of the heavenly Father, to redeem humanity from sin and death. Undoubtedly, the very first beats of the human Heart of Jesus were for His eternal Father, for the Immaculate Virgin who gave Him her most pure blood and her stainless flesh, and for guilty man whom He came to save. But side by side with these three great loves, we see born in that adorable Heart another inclination, a tender predilection, a powerful affection which will dominate the entire life of Jesus and of which He will never cease to give proofs.

Scarcely has He been conceived in the virginal womb of Mary, when He inspires His Mother to go in haste to the mountains and to enter the house of the priest Zachary. He is eager to communicate to John, still shut up in his mother's womb, purity without stain and most sublime sanctity. Who then is this child who attracts Him so powerfully, and to whom He grants in advance such loving favors? What is this love so ardent, which the Heart of Jesus cannot contain, and which wishes to pour itself forth with such divine liberality?

It is the love of Jesus for His priests, for this priesthood of which He Himself is the Head. Jesus—an eternal Priest according to the order of Melchisedech, a unique Priest in whom, and by whom alone, all other priests have power and dignity—loves with a love of predilection those whom He makes sharers in His priesthood. He loves them, and His Heart, throbbing with love, recognizes, in the child of Elizabeth, the mysterious link which is to unite the ancient priesthood which is about to disappear, to the new priesthood which He is about to institute. Thanks to John, the sacerdotal chain will not be broken. By him, the vigorous shoot, which will soon grow up on the old fallen tree of Aaron, will be able to draw its sap from the glorious past, while the fires of the Spirit of Love, and the divine dew of the Blood of Jesus, will make it bear admirable flowers and exquisite fruits. This love for priests was the attraction which led the Word Incarnate towards the child of Zachary and Elizabeth.

But, perhaps it will be said that John was not a priest. He did not succeed his father in the holy functions of worship. We do not see him in the temple offering incense at the appointed hour, or sacrificing the rams on the altar. He never tasted the flesh of the figurative victims immolated to Jehovah. Neither did he perform the functions of the Christian priesthood, he did not take his part at the supper of Jesus; he did not consecrate, he did not confer the vivifying sacraments of the new dispensation. All this is true, and nevertheless John is a priest; but, as he was to serve as a bond of union between the two priesthoods, it was fitting that he should not belong completely either to the one or to the other, and that nevertheless he should share in both.

The Evangelist seems to take pleasure in bringing out in relief the sacerdotal character of St. John, when he draws attention to the fact that not only Zachary, but also Elizabeth, was of the race of Aaron. The message of the coming conception of John was given to his father in the Temple, in the part reserved for the priests, at the time when Zachary, offering to the Lord the sacrifice of perfumes, was in the very act of the priesthood. John comes into the world. He soon retires to the desert, it is there that he grows up, separated from the rest of men, instructed by God Himself.

John is a priest. The temple where he fulfills the functions of his ministry is the desert. It is there, under the resplendent vault of the eastern sky, that the incense of his adorations and the harmonious hymns of his love ascend to God; it is there, that he offers a victim, more perfect, without doubt, than those of the Old Law, still less excellent than the divine Victim of the New Law, for this victim is himself, which he himself immolates by the sword of rigorous austerity, a victim at the same time bloody and unbloody.

John is a priest. Like the priests of the Christian priesthood, he announces the good news, he preaches penance, he shows the Saviour to souls, he instructs, he enlightens, he reproves. What a fine figure of a priest is John, so free from the bonds of this earth, so pure in his morals, so ardent for truth, so zealous for souls, so strong in the repression of evil! The rigor of the law of fear still made itself felt in his teaching which the benignity of Christ had not penetrated, but how humble and forgetful of himself he was, and how respectful and tender towards Jesus!

John was the precursor of Christ; are not all priests called to be, like him, precursors of Jesus? And is not the "Ecce Agnus Dei," which they repeat for the last nineteen centuries, a faithful echo of the word of the Baptist? (*John* 1:29).

It was then the profound and ardent love of Jesus for His priests which led Him to John, and which induced him to pour out the torrent of His graces into the soul of His precursor. When He purified him, sanctified him, filled him with joy from the womb of his mother, it was His priesthood which He purified in advance, which He separated from and elevated above the rest of humanity. And later on, when on the banks of the Jordan, He went and asked John to baptize Him and when He bowed down under his hand—it is true that it was in order to take the outward form of the sinner, and to make Himself like us—but it was also to render homage to His priesthood. This was a prelude to the adorable subjection which He was to have to His priests; to that obedience of love which He was to render to them, by putting Himself in their hands, and delivering Himself to their will.

It is to His priests that Jesus gave the first fruits of His Love in the person of John. What should be your consolation, priest of Jesus, to think that the first beats of His Sacred Heart have been for you! It is to you that He gave His graces in anticipation, it is on you that He has bestowed His most precious gifts. But what a stimulus is not this to urge you to love Him, to induce you to give to this adorable Master the first ardors of your youth, the first pulsations of the love of your hearts!

CHAPTER II

Love of Jesus for His Priests during His Hidden Life and Public Life

*J*ESUS loved His priests from the dawn of His existence, from the moment when the first lineaments of His Humanity were formed in the womb of Mary. And, as a vessel becomes saturated with and retains the perfume of the first liquid with which it has been filled, longer than of any other liquid that may be poured into it afterwards; so, the Heart of Jesus, from the beginning filled with love for His priests, for His Priesthood, has been penetrated with it more intimately, more profoundly than by any other love. All His life, He has allowed this tender inclination to show itself, He has allowed loving words to escape from His lips, He has never ceased to show the respect and love which He bore for His priests.

Of the long years of His hidden and silent life at Nazareth, but one incident has reached us. Having ascended to Jerusalem for the Feast when He was twelve years of age, Jesus remains, unknown to Joseph and Mary, in the holy town, and it is only after three long days of searching that they find Him there. It is in the Temple that Jesus remains. He is found there, not in adoration before the holy Ark, not standing near the altar where the fire consumes the victim, but with the doctors and priests listening to them and asking them questions. (*Luke* 2:46).

Later on, in the days of His public life, what respect does He not show for the Priesthood? One day, He cured a leper: "Go," said He to him, "show thyself to the priests." (*Matt.* 8:4; *Luke* 5:14; *Mark* 1:44). Render homage to them, recognize their authority, do their will, He seemed to add. When obliged, in order to enlighten the people, to stigmatize the vices and the personal degradation of the Jewish priesthood, formerly so great, but now fallen so low, the divine Master at the same time exalts the sacerdotal dignity and proclaims priests and doctors to be the dispensers of truth, and teachers of souls: "They have sitten on the chair of Moses. All things, therefore, whatsoever they shall say to you, observe and do; but according to their works do ye not." (*Matt* 23:2–3).

The Evangelist, inspired by the Spirit of Jesus, when reporting these words of Caiphas: "It is expedient for you that one man should die for the people" (*John* 11:50), draws our attention to the greatness of the sacerdotal character and the privileges which it confers: "Being the High Priest of that year, he prophesied." (*John* 11:51). In spite of his unworthiness, in spite of the sentiments of hatred and base jealousy with which he was animated, Caiphas, by the sole fact that he was high priest, received from God the gift of prophecy. He revealed by these few words, without knowing it perhaps, the marvellous economy of the mystery of the Redemption. Yes, even when the priest has fallen, even when sin debases him and sullies him, his dignity must still be respected, for God respected it even when He saw it lowered and debased in the person of Caiphas.

At the last hours of His life, Jesus still respects the ancient priesthood which is tottering on its foundation; He shows Himself deferential and respectful towards those who have constituted themselves His judges. Standing before the high priest, He listens to him and replies to him. His grave and measured words, His humble and modest countenance testify sufficiently that He sees in those who condemn Him a superior authority. No word of reproach escapes from His divine lips. He allows Himself to be beaten, He bows down, He pardons.

Oh, how well this adorable Master knows how to instruct the faithful! How well He knows how to show them to what limits they ought to carry their respect for the sacerdotal character! The priest has his weaknesses; he is a man. Let us throw a veil over his human miseries and raise our thoughts higher. Let us see the divine grandeurs hidden under lowliness and nothingness; let us see the action of Christ hidden under human shadows. And even when the fall is complete, let us still respect the priest; he has become a ruin, let us weep over the scattered debris; let us weep over that temple which God had chosen for His residence; over that temple which a holy anointing had consecrated, and which, now profaned and fallen, serves as a haunt for wild animals. Let us weep and pray.

If Jesus respected the Jewish priesthood, how much more has He not loved the Christian priesthood! He Himself chose it, He instructed it. He formed it with His own hands. It is His work of predilection, the work of His Heart.

Let us follow Jesus, step-by-step, during the three years of His public life; we shall see Him unceasingly occupied with the formation, the instruction, the perfecting of His priests. It is He who chooses them and who calls them to follow Him. His look, profound and sweet, that look which penetrates to the inmost depths of souls, fixes itself upon them. By His divine foreknowledge, He sees what they will be capable of and, in spite of their weakness and their present miseries, He raises them up to Himself. Some, called by Him, will retire after following Him; from the very start, the courage of others will give way before the sacrifices which this divine vocation imposes. The Heart of Jesus will suffer from these defections and from these acts of cowardice, and turning towards the faithful ones, the adorable Master will say: "Will you also go away?" (*John* 6:68).

After making the Twelve [Apostles] princes of His Church, He also separates from His ordinary followers seventy-two of the more faithful and more fervent, whom He marks for His Priesthood. He gives them His instructions; He opens the treasures of Heaven to adorn these new Apostles with admirable gifts and divine privileges (*Luke* 9:1; *Matt.* 10:1); then He sends them, two by two, to announce salvation to every creature. (*Luke* 10:1; *Matt.* 9:37).

When they return from their apostolic journeys, with what tenderness He welcomes them, with what maternal solicitude He invites them to repose: "Come," He says, "and rest a little." (*Mark* 6:31). To the crowds, He speaks in parables, veiling the brilliancy of the divine truths under the shadow of images, in order not to dazzle the feeble eyes of the multitude. But when His disciples ask Him in private for some explanations, with what affectionate sweetness He replies to their questions: "To you it is given to know the mysteries of the kingdom of Heaven." (*Matt.* 13:11). If He sees them terrified by the greatness of some of His miracles He says: Be of good heart, it it I, fear ye not." (*Matt.* 14:27).

The divine Master always speaks to them cheerfully and pleasantly, and with adorable kindness He clarifies their doubts and solves their difficulties. Attentive to their least wants, He seeks occasions to instruct them, fashioning them sweetly to those sacerdotal virtues of which He Himself is such a perfect model.

CHAPTER III

The Love of Jesus for His Priests at the Last Hours of His Life

*A*T THE LAST hours of His mortal life, Jesus reveals His love for His priests still more openly. In the discourse of the Last Supper, which John, the confidant of the divine Heart, has preserved for us, the tender love of the Master shines forth almost at every word: it is the revelation of the inmost designs of His Heart, the adorable effusion of His love: "With desire I have desired to eat this Pasch with you before I suffer." (*Luke* 22:15). His desire was to make His disciples sharers in His sacred priesthood, to mark them with that divine character by which they are raised above the Angelic hierarchies. He was in haste to place Himself in their hands under the Eucharistic form, to give Himself entirely to them, to depend on them. Like an artist who is impatient to see the masterpiece conceived in his imagination come to life under his hand, Jesus anticipated, by eager desires, the moment when He was to see the realized dream of His Heart: the Catholic Priesthood.

"With desire I have desired to eat this Pasch with you before I suffer." (*Luke* 22:15). Oh, I the ardent longing of the Heart of Jesus for His priests! He desired, with a great desire, to eat *this Pasch* . . . Several times already, He had eaten the Pasch with His disciples; but it was not *this Pasch* during which He was to institute His Priesthood. Like a father in the midst of his children, He presides at the repast; then He rises, and with exquisite humility, He kneels down before His disciples, and renders them the service of a slave, washing their feet and drying them gently. In order to diminish in some way the distance which separates them from Him, to raise up their courage, and render them less unworthy, even in their own eyes, of the favors of their divine Master,

He says to them: "You are clean." (*John* 13:10). He does still more. He raises them up to Himself, He establishes equality between them and Himself, He even goes so far as to assure them that: "Whoever receives him whom He shall have sent, receives *Himself.*" (*Matt.* 10:40).

The goodness of Jesus is displayed not only towards His faithful disciples, it extends even to him who betrayed Him. By warnings full of love, by affectionate words, He seeks to touch the heart of the traitor. He endeavors at least to instill into his heart the faith and the confidence which might bring him back after his crime.

The solemn moment has come. Infinite Love is going to produce a masterpiece; Infinite Wisdom and Infinite Power are going to co-operate in it. It will be the gift *par excellence* of divine Charity; it will be the Blessed Eucharist! God with us, God in us; Jesus Christ, God and man united, spirit to spirit, heart to heart, body to body, with man redeemed and purified: "Take ye and eat" says the Saviour. "Drink ye all of this." (*Matt.* 26:26–27).

But the effort of love is not completed. Jesus will not be always there in His human and perceptible form to work this great miracle. Other men invested with His power must succeed Him, and renew, during the course of centuries, the mysterious transubstantiation which He has just operated. Then it is that the Priesthood issues from the divine Heart. The privileged ones who surround Jesus at this hour, receive this sacred and indelible character which makes them priests for eternity, and which, the elect of love will bear from generation to generation, for the glory of their God and the salvation of the world.

Scarcely have the Apostles been invested with the sacerdotal character, when Jesus feels His love for them increase still more. He cannot contain it within Himself. He must needs give testimony of it to them: "You are they who have continued, with Me in My temptations. And I dispose to you, as My Father has disposed to Me, a kingdom." (*Luke* 22:28–29). Tender and caressing as a mother, He calls them "His little children." (*John* 13:33; *Mark* 10:24). He does not wish that they should give way to sadness: "Let not your heart be troubled, I go to prepare a place for you . . . I will come again and will take you to Myself." (*John* 14:1–3). "I will ask the Father, and He shall give you another Paraclete . . . I will not leave you orphans." (*John* 14:16–18). "He that loveth Me shall be loved by My Father." (*John* 14:21). Then by the comparison of the shoot and of the vine (*John* 15:5), He instructs them about this mysterious union which He establishes between them and Himself, which consists in the common possession of the one same priesthood. He urges them to make still closer this union, which is indispensable and without which they cannot bear fruit: "In this is My Father glorified; that you bring forth very much fruit . . . As the Father hath loved Me, I also have loved you. Abide in My Love." (*John* 15:8–9).

John the Baptist had given himself the sweet title of "Friend of the Bridegroom." Jesus had approved of it, and had with infinite grace used it Himself to indicate His Apostles on the day that He replied to the disciples of His Precursor: "The friends of the Bridegroom cannot fast and weep when the Bridegroom is with them." (*Luke* 5:34; *Matt.* 9:14–15). But, on this last evening, the divine Master, resuming this title, gives it solemnly to His priests, as the name which is proper to them: "You are My friends. I will not now call you servants . . . but I have called you friends." (*John* 15:13–15). What more tender and sweet than this title of "friends"? It is the special name of the object loved, of the object chosen by love. It may happen that a father, a brother, a spouse may not be loved at all; but a friend! He is a friend only because he is loved, and if he ceases to be loved, he ceases also to be called a friend.

The priest is, then, the special friend of Jesus. From the multitude of Christians whom He cherishes, the Master has marked him out and called him to His divine friendship. Thus, He says to His Apostles: "I have chosen you and have appointed you," and He adds: "I have chosen you out of the world." (*John* 15:16, 19). Yes, Jesus separates the priest from the multitude, but it is in order to elevate him higher, to favor him more, to unite him more intimately to Himself.

Finally, to complete His assurance of His divine love of preference for His Apostles and to raise up their courage, He assures them of the love of His heavenly Father: "The Father loveth you because you have loved Me." (*John* 16:27). "These things I have spoken to you, that in Me you may have peace. In the world you shall have distress; but have confidence, I have overcome the world." (*John* 16:33).

And behold! from His Heart, there bursts forth an ardent prayer. With His eyes turned towards Heaven, and His hands elevated, Jesus recommends to His Father the Priesthood which He has just established. He knows that He is soon going to leave this world, and that He will no longer be present in visible form among His Apostles to sustain them and console them. He knows also that they are weak and that, in the midst of the world where He sends them like sheep amidst wolves, they will be exposed to many sorrows and many dangers. (*Luke* 10:3). Thus, at this supreme hour, when the divine Redeemer is going, in a manner, to abdicate His divinity and His infinite power, in order to become an expiatory Victim, He feels the need of confiding to His Eternal Father interests so dear to His Heart: "It is for them that I pray," He says. (*John* 17:9).

Presently He will pray for His faithful, "for them also who through their word shall believe in Me." (*John* 17:20). But now He thinks only of His priests: "I pray not for the world, but for them whom Thou hast given Me." (*John* 17:9). He asks for them that perfect union of hearts and wills so necessary for the accomplishment of good; that union of view and action which alone is strength, and which is to permit His Church to pass through the floods of evil and the storms of persecution without growing faint: "That they may be one, as We also are one." (*John*, 17:22).

Finally, having many times repeated that His priests are not of the world—thus showing sufficiently by this insistence that, if they must live in the midst of the world, they must not, however, take its spirit or conform to its usages—Jesus, the divine Master, concludes with these exquisite words of humility, of vigilant tenderness: "And for them do I sanctify Myself; that they also may be sanctified in truth." (*John* 17:19).

When a mother wishes to teach her child to walk, she herself makes little steps before it such as it must make; and when, later on, she wishes to teach it to read, she also spells, in the manner of a child, the first words of the book. Jesus, who wishes His priests to be holy, sanctifies Himself amidst human weaknesses and necessities. He wishes them to be altogether like Himself, and He begins by making Himself altogether like them. He practices all the virtues for them. It is for this reason that He, the infinitely pure, subjects Himself to the prudent reserve which the watch over chastity demands; and that He allows Himself to be sometimes seized by sadness, in order to teach them to conquer similar temptations. He sanctifies Himself in order to serve as a model for them, to be the eternal exemplar of the Catholic priest, the finished type of sacerdotal perfection.

The hours have rolled rapidly by in this intimate self-revelation, during which the Heart of Jesus has shown itself so tender towards His disciples. The dolorous agony has come to break this Sacred Heart . . . . Nevertheless, Jesus rises and advances courageously before the cohort which is approaching to seize Him . . . Judas gives Him the kiss of betrayal. Jesus might have confounded the faithless disciple with a look, overwhelmed him with just reproaches, or crushed him with contemptuous silence; He does nothing of all that: on the forehead of the traitor He has seen the sacred character of the priesthood. He respects it still; He still loves this soul which He has elevated to such a height and which He now sees fallen so low: "Friend" He says to him, "whereunto art thou come?" (*Matt.* 26:50).

Some moments later, at the moment just when He is going to deliver Himself to His enemies, the divine Master again turns His Heart towards His dear disciples. For Himself, He accepts, He eagerly desires prison and chains; but for them, He wishes peace and liberty: "If therefore you seek Me, let these go their way." (*John* 18:8).

When Jesus, agonizing on the Cross in frightful tortures, allowed His thoughts to go towards His Apostles, towards His priests on whom He had conferred so many benefits, His Heart must have been filled with immense bitterness. Peter, whom He had made chief and Pontiff of His priesthood, had denied Him three times, saying with contempt: "I know not this man." (*Matt.* 26:70, 72, 74). Judas, in whom He had placed special confidence, had betrayed and sold Him, and now, rejecting His offer of mercy, had given himself up to despair and to death. With the exception of the faithful John, whom Jesus saw at the foot of His gibbet, all had cowardly abandoned Him; all had left Him defenseless and helpless in the hands of His executioners. . . . And He remained alone in unutterable sorrow . . . all alone . . . with His invincible love and His Heart filled with pardons.

CHAPTER IV

The Love of Jesus for His Priests after His Resurrection

EATH MIGHT, for a few hours, still the most loving Heart of Jesus, and prevent It from beating. But scarcely will the radiant dawn of the Resurrection have appeared; scarcely will life have entered triumphantly into the sacred Humanity of the Saviour, when love will cause His Sacred Heart to beat anew, and it will be love for His Priesthood which will first overflow from It.

The first words of Jesus to Magdalen, after He had made Himself known, are for His priests: "Go to My brethren and say to them: I ascend to My Father and to your Father, to My God and your God." (*John* 20:17). My brethren! He does not say: Go and tell My disciples, My Apostles. These words are too cold to content His Heart. "Go to My brethren" (*Matt.* 28:10), He repeats to the holy women. The betrayals, the ingratitude, the cowardice of the evening before are all forgotten. Oh, who can comprehend this love of Jesus for His priests?

The forty days which the Saviour is to pass on earth after His Resurrection will all be employed in the definite formation of His Church. Previous to that, He had given Himself to the people; He instructed them, He consoled them, He cured their maladies, and caressed their little children, He made Himself all things to all. Now, He seems to have taken up His life again, only in order to devote it to His Apostles. His words, His miracles, His blessings will be solely for them. He is going to invest them with His power, to grant them such great privileges that no creature will be able to equal them. He will raise them so high that the kings of the earth will have to bend before them, and that the Principalities of Heaven might well be envious of them. He will clothe them to such a point with Himself, He will

124

live in such a manner in them, that they will do the works which He has done, and even greater ones still. (*John* 14:12). Can greater love be conceived than that which devises and accomplishes a union so complete? After He had manifested Himself to the women whose humble courage and faithful attachment merited this loving preference, Jesus appeared to Peter. (*Luke* 24:34). That disciple, in spite of his fall, so painful to the Heart of the Master, is, nevertheless, the first to receive His divine blessing. It is because he is the chief of the new Priesthood, the supreme Pastor of the sheep of Christ.

On the evening of the same day, after instructing and consoling the two disciples on the road to Emmaus, and revealing Himself to them by the Eucharistic mystery, the Saviour comes to the Supper-room and appears in the midst of His united Apostles; His face is radiant and sweet; His words are full of joy and tenderness: "Peace be to you. . . . Why are you troubled?" (*Luke* 24:36–38). He shows them His hands and His feet bearing the imprint of the nails, and with divine simplicity, He asks them for something to eat in order to convince them completely of the reality of His Resurrection. (*Luke* 24:39–41). Then, when faith has penetrated into their souls, Jesus bends towards them, and, with His divine breath, He communicates to them the life-giving Spirit. (*John* 20:22–23).

In the days of Creation, God, having formed man from the slime of the earth, had vivified him by His breath (*Gen.* 2:7), and had given immortality to his soul. In the days of Redemption, this same all-powerful breath, coming from the lips of Christ, gives His priests the marvellous power of vivifying souls and of raising them from the death of sin: "Receive ye the Holy Ghost: whose sins you shall forgive, they are forgiven them, and whose sins you shall retain, they are retained." (*John* 20:22–23). This divine privilege gives His priests a sort of participation in the creative power of God! Eight days later, Jesus repairs to the Supper-room. By a loving condescension, He comes to satisfy the desires of the obstinate and incredulous disciple. "Thomas," says He to him sweetly, "come here and put in thy finger hither, and see My hands, and bring hither thy hand and put it into My side; and be not faithless, but believing." (*John* 20:27). Put thy hand into My Heart, the Master seemed to say to him, and feel Its beats of love. Could Thomas fail to recognize, by this trait of infinite goodness, the Heart of his Saviour and of his God?

One day, the Apostles, pressed by want, had taken again to their fishing boat and their nets, and had gone fishing on the beautiful lake of Tiberias, that had so often been witness of the miracles of Jesus. After a long night passed in fruitless labor, the morning had come. And lo! on the shore, at the first light of dawn, a form appears: it is the Master, the Christ they loved so much. His voice, sweet and grave, resounds over the waters, in the silence of nature still sleeping: "Children, have you any meat?" (*John* 21:5). How good the admirable Master shows Himself at this hour, and how fatherly! And when the Apostles come on shore, dragging the nets filled by miracle, they find a fire lighted, the meal prepared, and Jesus, as the least among them, arranging everything, and abasing Himself even to serving them Himself.

After the repast, Jesus approaches Peter. Is He going to reproach him for his falls? Is He going to take the primacy from him, to give it to one more worthy and more faithful? Is He going at least to put him on trial again, and bring home to him his own weakness? He will do nothing of the kind. His Heart is too delicate to make even an allusion to the past: "Simon," said He with incomparable tenderness, "Lovest thou Me more than these?" "Lord I love Thee." "Feed My lambs!" (*John* 21:15). That is to say, govern My faithful, be their chief and father, labor solicitously in providing nourishment for them. And Jesus resumes: "Simon, lovest thou Me?" "Yes, Lord." "Feed My lambs!" Be a mother to my faithful, bear them in your heart, nourish them with your own substance, give your life for them. And again Jesus asks: "Simon, lovest thou Me?" Had not two protestations been enough for the Master to convince Him of the love of His disciple? Doubtless, they had been enough, and that is why the care of ruling the faithful had been confided to Peter. But Jesus wishes to give still more to His Apostle. He wishes to confide to him the part of His flock dearest to His Heart, and for that, He demands a greater and stronger love.

Peter, saddened by this inexplicable insistence, replied: "Lord, Thou knowest all things, Thou knowest that I love Thee." (*John* 21:17). This response is not only an act of love, like the first two; it is also an act of firm faith in the divinity of Christ: "Thou knowest all things," and of absolute confidence in His Heart: "Thou knowest that I love Thee." That is what Jesus was waiting for. He says to Peter: "Feed My sheep!"

Be the chief, the shepherd, the pastor of My priests; lead them to the pastures of truth. Give your most vigilant care to these sheep that I love so tenderly; see that they be strong and fruitful, for it is by them that My flock is to increase.

Jesus had told His Apostles to betake themselves to a mountain in Galilee, and to assemble the whole flock of His disciples around them. All being gathered together, He appeared to them. This time, it is no longer to converse familiarly with the faithful eleven, that the Master has come, for a great act is about to be accomplished. He wishes that a great number of the faithful be witnesses of what He is about to do and be able to relate to future generations the immense liberality and the astounding gifts of grace and love which He is going to pour out on His priests. All have prostrated themselves before Him, and have adored Him. However, He does not address His words to the respectful and recollected multitude gazing at Him rapt in awe. He calls His Apostles, His priests, to Himself, and before these five hundred witnesses, He clothes them with His own power, and confers on them the most extraordinary privileges.

With that sovereign authority which belongs to Him, with that sweet, grave majesty which always surrounds Him, the Master pronounces these words of God: "All power is given to Me in Heaven and on earth. Going therefore, teach ye all nations, baptizing them in the name of the Father, and of the Son, and of the Holy Ghost, teaching them to observe all things whatsoever I have commanded you." (*Matt.* 28:18–20).

All power has been given to Me, and I associate you with My power. All that I have done, you shall do also: I give My powers to you. Go forth then! no longer as weak and powerless men, but as Christ's envoys, as the envoys of God. Go into the whole world and teach all the nations. Dispel the darkness of ignorance; fill men's intellects with truth, be masters of the world and teachers of souls. Be priests, ministers of the living God. Acting in the name of the entire Trinity, purify souls, transform them, raise them up to Heaven, by the power of the Father, by the wisdom of the Son, and by the ardent charity of the Holy Ghost. All those who believe your word, all those who submit themselves to your authority, shall be saved; all those who reject your teaching shall be condemned.

And Jesus concludes with these sublime words: "And behold, I am with you all days even to the consummation of the world." (*Matt.* 28:20). He does not address Himself to the multitude at this moment; He does not wish to speak here of the union by His grace with all Christians which He is to establish. Neither is there question of the general union which His Eucharistic presence produces, for all can approach the Tabernacle, all the faithful in the state of grace can nourish themselves with the divine Victim. It is of a grace of special union with His priests that Jesus intends to speak at this moment, a union so close, that the word of the priest is the very word of Christ: "He that heareth you heareth Me" (*Luke* 10:16), and that to dishonor the priest is to dishonor Christ: "He that despiseth you despiseth Me." (*Luke* 10:16). This is a union of love, by which Jesus not only draws the priest to Himself, but penetrates into him, lives in him, in order to make of him another Self; another Jesus in power over souls, in light in souls, in tender love for souls.

The forty days fixed by the Master are nearing the end; one last time, He comes to manifest Himself to His Apostles before going to take possession of His glory. He repairs to Jerusalem in the midst of them, and this time, putting aside His meekness and His usual indulgence, He reproaches them for their hardness of heart, their slowness in believing in the Resurrection, their pride and their cowardice.

It is still His love for His Apostles which suggests to Him to speak to them thus. He has just raised them to the most sublime dignity; He has just made them masters of the world; in a short time He is going to open their minds, giving them to understand the Scriptures; other admirable gifts will soon be communicated to them by the Holy Spirit. A counter-balance is needed to so many graces; they must be convinced of their human misery, so that they may not become proud and use the favors of their Master to exalt themselves like gods.

After revealing to them the sense of the Sacred Books and recalling to them what had been written of Him and what He had accomplished, He said to them: "It is you who are witnesses of these things." (*Luke* 24:48). "You shall remain in Jerusalem until you are clothed with power from on high. You shall receive the power of the Holy Ghost, coming upon you, and you shall be witnesses unto Me in Jerusalem, and in all Judea, and even to the uttermost part of the earth." (*Acts* 1:8).

Jesus places no bounds for the apostolate of His priests, He places no limits for their beneficent and divinizing action, except the extremities of the earth!

Having finished these words, the divine Master goes out with His Apostles and leads them to the Mount of Olives. He traverses once more with them those roads which they had followed together forty days before, on the evening of the Last Supper and where He had spoken those words overflowing with tenderness, which we have reported above. He crosses the garden of Gethsemane which witnessed His sorrowful agony. Once more He ascends the Mount of Olives.

Having arrived at the summit of the mountain, Jesus turns to His disciples. He looks at them with His profound, luminous gaze, penetrating to the very centre of their souls. His whole Heart, so ardent, so faithful, so tenderly good, passes into that look which He casts on His Apostles prostrated at His feet. He raises His hands to bless, and slowly, as if in regret to leave those dear disciples, in a pure sky illuminated by a springtime sun, He is lifted up. He ascends slowly, leaving the earth by degrees. Soon a luminous cloud commences to envelop Him; the Apostles now distinguish nothing but two hands stretched out which continue to bless; then all is lost in the light; Christ has entered into His glory.

CHAPTER V

The Love of Jesus for His Priests after His Ascension

W HEN SCARCELY formed in the womb of Mary, the Heart of Jesus had throbbed with love for His priests. The son of Zachary had been the first to feel Its divine influence and, as we have seen, the whole life of the Saviour was one long continuation of testimonies of this incomparable love. At the last hours of His life, and even in death, He loved His priests. After His Resurrection, He devotes Himself entirely to them, fills them with the most signal favors, and, in a manner, makes them equal to Himself.

But now that He has ascended into Heaven, what will He do? In the beatitude in which He reigns, in the eternal glory which belongs to Him by right, and to which, nevertheless, He has wished to attain by conquest, His Heart is not changed. What He loved during His life on earth, He loves always. He loves with an eternal love without change and without end.

Thus we see the adorable Master, at the moment of His departure from earth, leaving His priests a new pledge of His tender love. While He is ascending to Heaven, there falls from His blessed hands on His beloved disciples the gift of a remarkable grace, the precursor of the still more marvellous gifts which the Holy Spirit will soon communicate to them.

The inspired author expressly remarks, that, after the Ascension of their good Master, the Apostles left the Mount of Olives and returned to Jerusalem full of joy. (*Luke* 24:52). They had lost the visible presence of their Master, so consoling and so strengthening. Now they saw themselves alone, in face of a future full of persecutions and sufferings; without strength, without light, waiting full of uncertainty, charged with a crushing mission. Should not their hearts be filled with sadness, uneasiness, discouragement, and sorrow? and nevertheless they returned with souls inundated with joy!

This joy was the gift of the Heart of Jesus to His priests. It was not an illusory consolation, an earthly contentment, but a holy unction issuing from divine Charity and flowing from the hands of Jesus, to the very inmost recesses of the souls of His Apostles. It was, if we may so express it, sacerdotal joy.

The priest suffers, he suffers more than others, perhaps, since he must always live above himself, perpetually separated from all that is merely human. But, if he is faithful, he feels, nevertheless, at the bottom of his soul, a sentiment of supernatural joy, a tranquil serenity, a peculiarly sweet unction which, issuing from its inward source, extends even to his exterior. Ordinarily the faithful and fervent priest is joyful. Every morning when ascending the altar of sacrifice, he repeats with the Psalmist: "I will go in to the altar of God; to God who giveth joy to my youth." The purity of his life, the unction of sacerdotal joy do actually preserve his youth, and even in advanced age, the priest preserves a freshness of soul, a vivacity of sentiment, a delicacy of sensibility that other men cannot experience.

A single love fills the heart of the priest: the love of God! This unique and vivifying love cannot be mistaken. The priest is ennobled and guided by a single ambition: the glory of God! This noble ambition is never deceived. Thus, joy inundates his soul, and it is for him a first and magnificent recompense for the sacrifices which he has imposed on himself. It is a foretaste of the happiness promised to the valiant soldiers of Christ, and guaranteed to the special friends of the Saviour.

Ten days after the Ascension, the promised Consoler, the Spirit of Love Who proceeds from the Father and the Son, was sent by Jesus to His dear Apostles to accomplish His work in them, to complete their instruction; to enlighten them, to fortify and enrich them with the most excellent gifts. Infinite Love, on this day, keeps neither measure nor reserve. It flows in such abundance on the Priesthood, that Peter and his brethren were not only nourished and surfeited with grace, but they were actually inebriated with it, and so transported by love, that a single instant was enough to transform them into different men.

Since this ineffable gift of the Holy Spirit was made by Jesus to His priests, not a day, not an hour, perhaps, but has been marked by new proofs of the tender love of the Heart of Jesus for His priests. In the long succession of ages, we see this Infinite Love envelop the Priesthood, and the divine Master working with it, fighting with it, living in it.

During the long ages when Christian blood inundated the earth, priests were then in the first rank of martyrs, encouraging the weak, sustaining those who were wavering. How many Pontiffs and priests then received the palm of the victorious!

When the heresies appeared, the sacerdotal body was there to defend truth that was in danger. There were Gregories, Basils, Augustines who were inspired by Jesus, and raised as an invincible barrier before error and deception.

The Priesthood! How grand Jesus makes it in the person of Ambrose driving away the master of the world from the portals of his cathedral, and forcing him to bend the knee in penance! How powerful He makes it in a Leo, stopping with a gesture the inundating torrent of barbarians!

And during this period of transformation when a new civilization was being elaborated, it is still the priestly body that we see enlightening by its learning the nations in the process of formation and the new peoples. How many great Pontiffs have occupied the chair of Peter! How many saintly bishops have carried into all kingdoms, with the Christian faith, the splendor of the Gospel morality! Later on, it is the voice of a Pontiff and the voice of a priest that set all Europe in motion and sent it, enthusiastic and quivering with emotion, to the conquest of the tomb of Christ.

Sacred Theology, philosophy, the arts and even the sciences received a new impulse from the Priesthood. We see the immortal writings of St. Thomas of Aquinas and of St. Bonaventure come to life under its vivifying breath, at the same time as the marvellous architecture of our Gothic cathedrals.

Side by side with the sciences and the arts, the most sublime virtues shine, and if we follow the course of the centuries, we shall see Jesus constantly lavishing on His Pontiffs and priests His choicest divine favors. He crowns the Priesthood with every glory; He gives to it the empire over souls; He makes it great, powerful, devoted, charitable and merciful like Himself. He makes it humble in persecutions, courageous in suffering, strong against the enemies of the Faith, ardent in the pursuit of souls. At different epochs, to meet ever-changing circumstances, He sends St. Dominic and his preachers; the humble and destitute sons of St. Francis; the knight-priest, St. Ignatius, and his chosen troop; St. Philip Neri and the saintly priests who follow him; the great bishop of Milan uniting to the Cardinal's purple the poverty of Christ and the austerities of the anchorites; the Bishop of Geneva, the gentle and the strong, the master of piety and the doctor of Love.

To mention only France, so fertile in great and holy works during these centuries, we find St. Vincent de Paul filled with the charity of the Saviour, and that phalanx of saintly priests, the Berulles, the Olliers, the Condrens, and the fervent disciples whom they form. We see the great orators making truth shine from the Christian pulpit, and that crowd of valiant missionaries, sent forth from all the nations, making new Christian communities spring up on every shore by their sweat and blood.

During the dark days of the French Revolution, to how many faithful priests has not Jesus granted the honor and the grace of shedding their blood for His Name? Others take the road of exile; others still, with admirable devotedness, expose their lives for the salvation of souls.

And during this great century which has just ended, has Jesus closed His hands and stopped the course of His gifts? We see admirable Pontiffs crowned with the tiara; Pius IX filled with the goodness of the Saviour; so great in misfortune, so patient and so strong in disaster, proclaiming the doctrine of the Infallibility, and of the Immaculate Conception; and Leo XIII enlightening the world by the light of his immortal Encyclicals, a king without territory, without treasury and without army, dominating all the kings of the world and becoming arbitrator between them.

In Germany, in Italy, in France, everywhere, Bishops, worthy successors of the Apostles, resist with the strength of Christ the aggression of revolution, delivering themselves to the buffets of the impious to defend the sheep of the fold. We see some of them die on the barricades or under the fire of the enemies of God, holy victims immolated for the people.

And so many priests founders of works of zeal; so many campaigners of the word, so many fervent and pious! And those last; the little and the unlearned: the Vianneys, the Eymards, the Chevries, the Cottolengos, the Don Boscos, and so many others favored by Jesus, the Friend of the humble, with the most marvellous gifts, and elevated by Him to such a high degree of sanctity!

Oh, how much Jesus has loved His priests! How many proofs of His immortal love He has given them during the nineteen centuries which have elapsed since His entry into glory! The divine Master has not ceased for a single moment to live in His priests, and it is His divine virtues, it is His luminous intellect, it is the splendors of His Soul and the goodness of His Sacred Heart which we have seen alternately shine in them. Jesus has poured forth His Soul, He has communicated His Heart to His priestly body; it is He who, during the centuries, has made priests so grand! It is He who has made them so pure, so good, so charitable and so enlightened!

CHAPTER VI

The Love of Jesus for His Priests at the Present Time

So MANY ineffable gifts of love have not exhausted the infinitely loving Heart of Jesus. At the dawn of the twentieth century, He loves His priests as ardently and tenderly as when He formed them with His hands, or when, having instructed them by His word and His shining example, He sent them to the conquest of souls.

From His throne above, from the depths of His solitary and too often abandoned tabernacles, our adorable Saviour has seen humanity, led astray by a false idea of independence, shake off the beneficent yoke of His law and depart from the straight path. He has seen waves of evil rise up and threaten souls. He has seen materialistic idolatry and the worship of human reason replace in the mind of man, faith in the Eternal Creating Being, knowledge of his own nothingness and hope of his immortal destiny. He has seen cold egoism and wretched selfish motives, like a malignant cancer, eat away the heart of man, which was created for a love that is infinite, and for unbounded generosity and self-sacrifice. He has seen skepticism, the negation of all supernatural action, thirst for gold, and the degradation of impurity, act as powerful solvents on all human societies, and, breaking all bonds, tear asunder and destroy the family, social fraternity, and the homogeneity of nations.

He has seen the world tottering on its foundations, and seized by immense pity for the human race redeemed by His Blood, for the ungrateful human race which is turning away from Him, He has leaned towards His priests and said to them: Come to Me, My faithful ones, My beloved; come and help Me to reconquer souls! Behold! I send you again to teach the nations; bring salvation to them by the truth of your words and by the light of your example.

And as you will have to fight and will have to suffer; as you will work for My glory and will give Me souls, *I bestow on you a gift which is precious among all gifts. I give you My Heart!* I give It to you as a sword and a buckler for the combat; as a guide and light in your ways; as a consoler in your sorrows. Draw without fear from the treasures of love which It contains. Draw first for yourselves, enrich yourselves with Its plenitude; fill your hearts with it, until they overflow. Then draw for others; pour My love into souls; carry everywhere this divine fire which is to purify and to renew the earth! *And Jesus drawing the priests to His divine breast, gives them His adorable Heart the pledge of His incomparable love.*

But the divine Master thought that, perhaps, He would not be heard by all, and that people would doubt His word. Then He drew from His Heart a gift of love visible to all eyes. He granted to His Priesthood another new grace, this time apparent and tangible.

A great light had just disappeared from the ecclesiastical firmament; a great Pope had descended into the tomb, and the world was in expectation. The children of the world, in their foolish presumption, were naming in advance, according to their own inclination, the successor of Peter. The faithful prayed, the Cardinals in their uncertainty sought the chosen one of the Lord. But the Holy Spirit, the Spirit of Love, hovered over the conclave, and His divine influence caused the name of Joseph Sarto to be drawn from the sacred chalice. The world remained struck with astonishment, and the Church knelt to receive from the hand of Jesus Christ, the Vicar whom He had chosen.

The Sacerdotal body quickly understood what an ineffable gift the Heart of Jesus conferred on them by giving them as father and guide the Patriarch of Venice. Who better than he would be able to rule the flock of Christ: the lambs and their mothers? Who better than he, could comprehend both the greatness of the priest, and the difficulties which he meets with, and the forms which his apostolate may take, and the needs of his soul and his heart?

The son of a humble family, like the greater number of priests, the new Pope had lived in his youth the austere and studious life of poor scholars. He had raised himself above his condition by the brilliancy of his intellect. Later on, he owed his entry into the seminary, like so many others, to charitable patronage. Then he had followed all the degrees of the priesthood. He had known the humble dependence and the fatigues of being assistant priest, the solitude of a small country parish, the frugal and devoted life of a small village pastor. For long years he had, from the sole motive of the glory of his God, given the best of himself to the souls confided to his care.

Then the light that was within became visible to the discerning. Distinguished from others by his strong and amiable virtues, he had ascended, step-by-step, the higher degrees of the hierarchy, and, always constant and even-tempered, as modest under the mitre of the Bishop and under the purple of the Cardinal, as in the humble position of village pastor, he had shown himself as the model of the priest, of the priest according to the Heart of God; fervent in prayer, devoted to the interests of Jesus, zealous for the truth, clothed with the goodness and humility of the Saviour, chaste and austere in his life, merciful to sinners, filled with love for Jesus, his adorable Master, for Mary, his Immaculate Mother, for the Church and for souls!

And scarcely has this Chosen one taken his seat on the chair of Peter, when, urged by a divine inspiration, he issues an appeal to the priests of the world. In his first Encyclical, in his first words addressed to the world, does not Pius X allow the ardent love of his heart for priests to appear? Like Jesus, his divine Master, he wishes them to be holy, zealous, fervent and devoted to souls. He wishes them to be superior to all in learning, but above all, in virtue. He wishes them to be filled with that apostolic fire of the first priests formed by Jesus. We feel in the words of Pius X: a heart smitten by the grandeur and the beauty of the Priesthood; a heart resolved to guard with the utmost solicitude this noblest and dearest part of his flock. Is not this father, this pastor of the sheep of Christ, a gift of love from the Heart of Jesus to His priests?

The divine Master has given them this visible testimony of His love. In the gift of His Sacred Heart, He has given them the ineffable cup, the divine chalice from which Infinite Love gushes forth. What further could He give them? Doubtless nothing. But what He can do, is, to continue always giving Himself; to continue to press more closely to His Sacred Heart His priests whom He has loved so passionately for twenty centuries; to make them always more like Himself, always more worthy of His immortal love.

At the beginning of Part III of this book, we have compared the love of the Heart of Jesus to a stream with profound and limpid waters. We have taken pleasure in going up to its source and in seeing the love for the Priesthood issue from this divine Heart from the first moment of Its conception. It has never ceased since then to flow from it. The passionate and tender love of Jesus for His priests has always continued to flow from this Sacred Heart in royal abundance.

We have endeavored to follow the course of this stream of love across the centuries. How sweet it would be for us to sit down on its banks, to rest there a long time and to contemplate for long hours the clear reflection from its waves! But we must pass on.

This divine stream will still flow on, fertilizing everything along its banks. The fidelity of holy priests in corresponding with the love of Jesus, their admirable virtues, their devotedness and their purity are the tributaries by which it will be swelled, and it will finally precipitate its dazzling sheet of water into the immense ocean of eternal Love.

And the love of Jesus for His priests will never have an end! After giving them, in time, jurisdiction over souls, He will take them as His assessors at the Last Judgment, and during all eternity they will remain with Jesus, the eternal Priest and the eternal Victim, always priests and always victims to their God. In the company of the Lamb ever immolated, they will be for all eternity as a perpetual sacrifice of praise and adoration before the supreme Majesty of God.

Perpetually also, Infinite Love, to which they will render honor and glory, will fill them with Its gifts, and because they have worked on earth to spread its burning flames, It will inebriate them for all eternity with Its chaste and divine delights!

O Jesus, our sweet mercy, with what love does not Thy Heart burn for Thy priests! They are the object of Thy ineffable tenderness, of Thy divine solicitude. Thou dost draw them to Thee with words so sweet, with complaints so touching! Like a tender lamb, wounded by the malice of men, Thou moanest sweetly to call those who can comfort and cure Thee. Thou hast thirst for love, Thou hast thirst for souls, and Thou dost extend Thy parched lips towards those who can quench Thy thirst.

Thy priests! It is to them, divine Jesus, that Thou dost come to seek consolation for Thy Sacred Heart. It is in them that Thou dost wish to find all that the world refuses to Thee: fidelity, devotedness, confidence and love. It is by them that Thou dost wish to carry out all that Thy divine Charity has resolved to accomplish for the salvation of mankind. It is by their voice that Thou dost wish to call the world to Thee; by their arms that Thou dost wish to embrace men and clasp them to Thy Breast; by their works and their sweat that Thou dost wish to fertilize the earth; by the ardor of their love that Thou dost wish to warm the world again. It is on them that Thou dost count to conquer evil; it is from them that Thou dost wish to receive the glory of triumph! O Jesus, merciful Goodness, how Thou dost love Thy priests!

✠ PART IV ✠

*Sublime Reflections on Infinite Love
and the Priesthood*

I

The Abysses of the Infinite Love

O PRIEST of God! privileged one of Infinite Love, come and contemplate the abysses of divine Charity, and if you can, sound their depths!

See first an immense abyss, so vast that no created eye can take it in; it is *Love-Creator*. Infinite Love had need of diffusing Itself outside Itself and It had resolved on the creation of man in order to be able to pour Itself out on him. And as a young mother lovingly prepares with her own hands the cradle for the child to which she is about to give birth; as she endeavors to make it, not only sweet and comfortable, but also graceful and pleasant-looking; so, Almighty God, who was to be at the same time father and mother, lovingly prepared man's cradle, the universe. He took pleasure in enriching it and adorning it with all that could contribute to the utility, to the service and the joy of His beloved creature.

At times, Almighty God stopped in His work and considered what was already done. He saw that nothing was wanting to it and found that all was good. (*Gen.* 1:31). Finally, when the great palace of the universe was arranged to receive the royal guest for whom it had been prepared, God created man, and in him Infinite Love was well pleased. The Most Holy Trinity having deliberated, man was formed, and the divine breath, the Spirit of God, Love, gave him life, a natural life of the body and the supernatural life of the soul, a life perfect and pure, life such as God made for man.

Contemplate next the second abyss. Man had sinned. He had transgressed God's commandment, and, as a rebellious creature, he deserved punishment. Infinite Sanctity demanded its rights. Justice was about to strike this being which had responded to the liberality of Love-Creator only by disobedience and pride. But Love, *Love-Mediator*, placing Itself between man, the sinner, and outraged God, formed a profound abyss, and Justice could no longer reach man to punish him.

For long centuries, Love-Mediator preserved the sinful creature from the thunderbolts of divine justice. It guided the Patriarchs and revealed Itself to them; It spoke by the Prophets; It preserved the true notion of God in the chosen people; It labored to prepare the entire human race for the work of the Redemption.

A third abyss of love now opens before you, so vast, so profound, so incomprehensible, that an incomprehensible love alone can explain it; it is *Love-Redeemer.*

The Word became incarnate. He had visited the earth, He had revealed to man the hidden mysteries of salvation. He had given all His Blood, and in this bounteous laver, culpable humanity had been washed. All the life of Jesus, all His adorable immolations culminated in that. The Love-Priest had offered the Love-Victim; the world was redeemed, divine Justice was disarmed, definite reconciliation between the Creator and the creature was effected. Jesus had died to give us life; when risen again, He had completed the formation of His Church; now He ascended again to His Eternal Father.

A new abyss of love opens before us; it is *Love-Illuminator.* The Holy Spirit, the Spirit of God, the substantial Love of the Father and of the Son, has descended upon the Church to fertilize it, as He had formerly fertilized the virginal womb of Mary. The Church has given birth to numerous children, and the Holy Spirit continues to enlighten it. Mysteries are revealed more clearly; souls, warmed by Love, serve God as He wishes to be served, "in spirit and in truth." (*John* 4:23). The word of the Apostles, the blood of the Martyrs, the teaching of the Doctors, the decrees of Councils, these living lights, the Saints, come, each at the appointed moment, raised up by Love-Illuminator, to complete the marvellous adornment of the divine Spouse of Christ.

Behold, now, a fifth abyss of Love! The times are accomplished. A new Heavens and a new earth have appeared (*2 Peter* 3:13; *Isaias* 65:17; *Apoc.* 21:1) and *Love-Glorifier* is about to crown the Elect. Nothing is wanting to the divine plenitude; all creatures have entered into the bosom of the Father, and Love, by glorifying them, glorifies Itself. An immense abyss, it contains all beings. Like a torrent of divine delights, it inundates all the blessed, and like a consuming and avenging fire, it devours the accursed. Love reigns as sovereign and undisputed Master.

It has done its work; It has gained the victory; all glory is rendered to It eternally! O priestly soul! do you not perceive still another abyss, the proportions of which no human word can express, and no created intelligence can measure? It is *Love without form,* Love without exterior manifestation, it is *God* Himself! Prostrated on the edge of this unfathomable abyss, adore in silence, and listen to a voice saying to you: "Infinite Love envelops, penetrates and fills all things. It is the only source of life and of all fruitfulness. It is the eternal principle of beings and their eternal end. If you wish to possess life and not be sterile, break the bonds which bind you to yourself and to the creature, and plunge into this abyss."

II

Love of God for Man, and of Man for God

G od is love! He loves from eternity to eternity!
 While Infinite Love, exercising Itself in Itself, takes pleasure in the marvellous communion which goes from the Father to the Son, and from the Son and the Father to the Holy Spirit; in that ineffable communication which the three divine Persons make to each other of the same Love which is their essence and their being; this Infinite Love acts outside Itself also; and as the proper action of love is to love, It loves every creature, every work that has issued from Its powerful word, all that was, all that is, and all that will be.

God loves! That is what He occupies Himself with in the sovereign possession of His Being and in the serene peace of His immortal glory. He loves! That is His life, His action, His pleasure, His divine food and His ineffably sweet repose. He loves! He wishes to love, He must continue to love. His love is Himself, and if He ceased to love, He would suddenly cease to be God.

God is Love! He gives love without reckoning. He pours it out with inexhaustible abundance on the entire creation. Nothing escapes from this divine deluge which strives to engulf everything.

God loves! But He wishes to be loved: love has need of a return. If, in the very bosom of the Divinity, the Father, the Word and the Holy Spirit give such a perfect return that They love each other with the same Love which is their essence, so Infinite Love wishes to find outside of Itself a reciprocity, doubtless relative and proportioned to the weakness of the created being, but nevertheless real.

God pours out torrents of love upon the creature; in his turn, the creature should love. God has deposited in each one, by the fact of its creation, a principle of love, not however in the same degree, or in the same form. In all justice and in all necessity, each creature should love according to its nature and the will of its Creator. It has received everything from God; it ought to give everything back to God; it is what it is only by God; it ought to employ its whole being for God.

This first love, this necessary love of the creature has, as it were, two movements. The first, a movement of restitution: the creature gives something to God, it returns it to Him. The second is a movement of submission: it accomplishes the will of its Creator.

We see this manner of loving admirably exercised by the inferior creatures. The earth has received its fertility from God, and it is constantly producing for its Creator. The flower has received the brilliancy of its calyx and the sweetness of its perfume; it flowers each spring for its God and it gives Him back its beauty and its fragrant odor. The bird has received its light wings and the sweetness of its song; and it flies, and it sings in the presence of its God. The wild animals that people the deserts have received from their Creator swiftness for running, strength for defense and beautiful covering; and they increase before God, according to the law of their nature, accomplishing the divine will and multiplying according to the good pleasure of their Master. This regular fulfillment of the divine will, and this renewed gift of what they have in themselves is the only way which these inferior creatures have of expressing their love.

But God has formed creatures of a higher order. In them also He has placed the principle of love; and as they have received more from divine munificence, they are bound to give more in return. In their case, God is no longer satisfied with that love of nature and instinct which the inferior beings give Him. As He has endowed them with reason, He expects from them a rational love; as He has given them free will, He expects from them voluntary love; as He has created them according to His image, He expects from them a love like His own.

God has given man not only that principle of love which He has given to inferior creatures, and by which he was already bound instinctively to tend towards God, and to submit himself to Him, but He has given him much more. He has formed in him a soul endowed with intelligence and free will, and by means of these faculties, man can enter into the knowledge of his Creator and develop in his heart a superior love, a love sovereignly reasonable and truly worthy of God. It is this enlightened love, this voluntary love which man owes to God. Why then does he not give this love to God? Why then is love so little understood by the human heart? I say the true love, the pure love, the supernatural love desired by God, which has descended from Him and which ought to go up again to Him; love, not such as the depraved mind of the fallen creature has conceived it, but as Infinite Love expects from the rational creature; a love finite and created, doubtless, like the creature himself, but enlightened, free and strong.

Nevertheless, few men love God as He wishes to be loved! Man's senses, radically impaired by sin, have lost the clear notion of truth. They go astray, they are deceived, they take the wrong road; man has no longer that beautiful luminous intellect, that firm, upright will which he had in the first days of his creation. He is the slave of ignorance and concupiscence. Thus we see him easily turned away from truth, changing the order of things, transforming good into evil, and often preferring evil to good: man's judgment has no longer its primeval rectitude, it is warped and too often it goes astray. Since his first sin, man has fallen into many errors; but perhaps on no point has he been so much deceived as on love. According as he became detached from God, he became more attached to creatures; and in an attempt to satisfy his heart, which hungered after Infinite Love, he gave it as food this purely earthly attachment and called it "love."

Man, forgetting God, no longer uniting himself to Him by love, no longer knowing what to believe, not daring to hope for anything, found himself in the midst of the world, like a poor shipwrecked man lost in the ocean. He tried to seize everything that presented itself to him, he attached himself to the smallest floating spar, and clinging to it like a man in desperation, he pressed it to his heart and persuaded himself that he loved it.

But that was not love . . . True love, the only love which deserves this divine name, is that which ascends to God, the only principle of love. Earthly lust, carnal pleasures, are passions unchained by original sin; they are the results of sin. They will never satisfy the intellect and the heart of man; they will never be love!

The intellect and the heart of man are two marvellous instruments created by God! Touched by the divine breath of Infinite Love, they should, in perfect accord, give forth the most pleasing harmony and, in a certain manner, gathering together all the notes sent up to Heaven by the inferior creatures, should form them into a melodious hymn of praise, gratitude and adoration.

All the moral beauty of man, the human harmony which should go up from him to Heaven, consists in this accord, in this perfect equilibrium between his intellect and his heart which it conserves and sustains. A single hand, a single breath, should make them vibrate at the same time, and Infinite Love alone is the divine instrument capable of touching these harmonious instruments which He Himself has created.

III

Double Movement of Infinite Love

G OD is Love! This Love, which is His essence, causes, at the
same time, both the Unity of His nature and the Trinity of His
Persons. This Infinite Love living and vivifying, living in Itself and by
Itself, and vivifying outside itself, not only tends to communicate by
its very nature, but It is, by the fact of the intensity of Its life and of
Its, immortal fertility, communication Itself. Infinite Love, because it is
living and fruitful, is a movement.[6] This movement takes place in God
by the communication of the Three Persons. It is like an uninterrupted
circulation which goes from the Father to the Son and to the Holy
Spirit. It is a unique vital movement, so compressed and so intense, that
at first sight it would seem to be an immobility.

This movement of love manifests itself externally as well. The most
marvellous production of its exterior movement of love is the humanity
of Jesus. The interior movement does not tend to any creation, to any
new production; it is a movement of repose and of enjoyment, a complete movement which can neither increase, nor diminish, nor change.
It is the plenitude of love which contents itself in a perpetual and always
equal movement between the three divine Persons.

The exterior movement tends to creation, to an incessant production. It is a movement of work, which contents itself by a perpetual
production of graces, of gifts, of spiritual life, and of creations and

---

6.   Mother Louise Margaret evidently takes the word *movement* here in the sense of activity and
not of change. She makes her meaning perfectly clear later on, when she says that in God this
movement is "a movement of repose and fruition."

It is interesting to see how St. Thomas, in his commentary on *De Trinitate* (quaest. 3, art.
4, ad 2ᵘᵐ and in his *Summa Theologica* Ia pars, quaest. 9, art ad 1ᵃᵐ) explains that one may, by
metaphor, speak of movement in God, as also Plato, St. Augustine, Denys, and Sacred Scripture itself have done. St. Thomas remarks that this metaphor of movement is applied both to
the immanent operations of the divine intellect and will and to the productive action.

(Note from French Edition published by the Central Council of the *Work of Infinite
Love.*)

material lives. These two movements, or rather this single movement is not less fruitful in the one than in the other of its forms: it is fruitful in God, by the eternal generation and the eternal procession; it is fruitful outside God, by grace and creation.

IV

Divine Charity

"*T*HAT being rooted and founded in charity, you may be able to comprehend with all the saints, what is the *breadth and length, and height, and depth.*" (*Ephes.* 3:17–18).

The Charity of God, which is immense and infinite, could not be measured by the human eye or by the gaze of the soul. Then the Being, Love, condensed, in a certain manner, this divine Charity, and, in the Heart of the Word Incarnate, has rendered It visible. Created beings have been able to see in this Heart, created, but adorable and divine, "the *breadth and length, the height and the depth of the Infinite Love.*"

Breadth: because it embraces the multitude of beings. There is not a single creature which Infinite Love does not nurse in its arms; not a single one that It has not willed, looked on with consideration, and loved; not one which It has not endowed and provided with all that constitutes its form and its existence.

There is first of all the angel, a pure creature, an immaterial spirit, a flame of living fire. Then there is man, uniting in himself the immortal, intelligent, rational, free soul to the material form of a body of flesh; a creature worthy of admiration, enveloping with a passable, mortal veil, a spiritual soul, a created light, vivified by the divine life.

Then there is the animal, by the blessing of God increasing and multiplying, and guided surely by its instinct towards its end. Next there is the tree of the forest, each spring feeling the vivifying sap ascend its century-old trunk and escape in the form of green buds; and the grass of the field, bending beneath the wind, and growing luxuriantly for the glory of its Creator. Finally, lowest in the scale, are the inert bodies, receiving from the divine Principle their form and brilliancy.

Length: it is the duration without limit of this Love. One day, creatures began to receive the Love of God, and that day was the day of their creation; but in God, love for the creature has never had a beginning. He bore their *idea exemplaris* in Himself from all eternity. He loved them then, long before creating them. He loved them as soon as He had conceived them in His mind. But did He conceive them some day? Has He not borne their *idea exemplaris* in Himself as long as He is God? And when did He begin to be God? . . . From all eternity, without beginning, Infinite Love has enveloped all creatures. Will it cease one day to love them? Never! The love of God is immutable and without change. What He has loved once, He loves always, and if sometimes He strikes and seems to destroy, it is always love which guides. He has loved from all eternity, He will love for all eternity.

Length! . . . Who will measure the length of this Infinite Love? Who will place a beginning for it, or assign an end? *Length!* He has always loved, He will always love, for all eternity.

Height! Infinite Love has ascended to incomprehensible heights. In the Father, it ascends even to the generation of the Divine Word, the omnipotent Word, the Eternal Wisdom, the only Son, in everything equal to the Father. It ascends in the Father and the Son even to the procession of the Holy Spirit, the principle of all love and all sanctity, God, like the Father and the Son. It ascends in the divine Trinity even to forming the most perfect unity; so that the Father and the Son and the Holy Ghost, are only one Love, one God in three Persons. It ascends in this one God even to the idea of creation, even to the accomplishment of this great work, even to the divine liberalities with which creatures have been favored.

This divine Love appeared in its sublimity when It conceived the idea of the Incarnation; when, after the fall of man, It disarmed Justice; when, in spite of incessant sins, It preserved Its merciful patience. This Love was sublime when the Word became incarnate; when He became a little infant, poor, humiliated, suffering; when He lived among us in the simplicity and goodness and gift of the whole Self! It was sublime, when He was in a death-agony in the Garden at the sight of our iniquities; when He appeared bound with chains, scourged, mocked, crucified! Sublime, in the Tabernacle, where He is chained as a prisoner during the ages; in the Holy Sacrifice, in which He immolates Himself, in the Blessed Eucharist, in which He makes Himself our food!

O the *sublimity* of the Infinite Love of God! Who will be able to raise himself up to Thee to comprehend Thee!

Depth! And who will be able to descend to Thy unfathomable depths? Infinite Love, this marvellous edifice composed of Omnipotence, infinite Wisdom, sovereign Goodness, unchangeable Justice, divine Mercy, absolute Good, perfect Beauty, has foundations so deep that nothing has ever been able to shake them. Time, which destroys everything, is of no avail against it. The tide of human iniquities has come and broken itself at its foundation, as the wave in fury breaks itself at the foot of the granite rock. All eternity will not be sufficient for the elect to penetrate to the lowest depths of the abyss of Love!

Depth! Let us go to the Heart of Jesus. Through the wide opening which the lance has made in It, let us look into this abyss of divine Charity; let us seek to sound its depths. But no! Thy soul is seized with dizziness before this abyss of Love. One must shut one's eyes, abandon every support, and let oneself fall, fall, fall without end in these divine depths, without seeking to understand, without wishing to explain: Love is not explained! It is desired, it is wished for, it is tasted, we are inebriated with it, we live on it, we die of it: we do not understand it. O, the depths. . . !

V

Infinite Love Humanized

S T. JOHN, wishing to convey to us an idea of the divine Being, wishing to sum up in a single term all the grandeurs, all the beauties, all the attributes of God, said: "God is Charity"! (*1 John* 4:16), "God is Love"! And if we wish to depict Jesus Christ, God and Man, in a single word; if we wish to include in a single term all that He is, all that He has done, and the very reason for His Being, we can say: Jesus Christ is His Heart, is His Sacred Heart.

Divine Charity, Infinite Love, is God whole and entire; God, what He is in Himself, and what He does outside of Himself; God, with His power, His justice, His wisdom; God who is, God who creates, God who redeems, God who enlightens and who recompenses. It is God without division, without exclusion, without reserve, splendidly summed up in a splendid phrase: "Deus caritas est." (*1 John* 4:16).

The Sacred Heart is Jesus Christ whole and complete, God and Man, the Word Incarnate. It is not only His Heart of flesh beating in His Breast, that meek and humble Heart, which we adore as the symbol or the organ of His incomparable love, it is His whole Being, divine and human; His Divinity, His Soul, His Body, each of the sacred Members; all His thoughts, His acts, His divine words. The Sacred Heart is God made man; it is Jesus Christ humiliated, delivered up, expiring; It is Jesus-Eucharist, ineffable victim of love, Jesus immolated on the altar, Jesus a prisoner in the Tabernacle.

God is explained completely and entirely by this word: *Charity,* for love explains everything although itself inexplicable. Jesus is completely explained by this name: The Sacred Heart! His sublime devotedness, His goodness, His mercy, all His divine virtues, His sacrifice, His death; His love explains all these. The Sacred Heart is divine Charity incarnate, Infinite Love humanized.

VI

The Blessed Eucharist and the Sacred Heart

*T*HE devotion to the Blessed Eucharist and the devotion to the Sacred Heart are two sister devotions. They are so intimately united, they complete each other so perfectly, that the one calls for the other, as if necessarily. Not only can the first of these devotions not prejudice the second; but they augment each other reciprocally, because they complete each other and perfect each other.

If we have devotion to the Sacred Heart of Jesus we shall try to find It in order to adore It, to love It, to offer to It our reparations and our praises; and where shall we seek It, if not in the Blessed Eucharist where It is found living eternally? If we love this adorable Heart, we shall desire to unite ourselves to It, for love seeks union; we shall wish to warm up our hearts again with the burning heat of this divine fire.

But to reach this Sacred Heart, to take hold of It, to put It in contact with our own, what shall we do? Shall we scale Heaven to carry away the Heart of Jesus triumphant in Its glory? Doubtless, we shall not. We shall go to the Blessed Eucharist, we shall go to the Tabernacle, we shall take the white Host, and when we have enclosed It in our breasts, we shall feel the divine Heart truly beating beside ours.

Devotion to the divine Heart infallibly leads souls to the Blessed Eucharist, and faith and devotion to the Blessed Eucharist necessarily lead souls to discover the mysteries of Infinite Love of which the divine Heart is the organ and the symbol. If we believe in the Blessed Eucharist we shall believe in love; it is the mystery of love. But love is, in itself, immaterial, and imperceptible. To fix our minds and our senses we seek a form for love; this form, this sensible manifestation is the divine Heart.

The Sacred Heart, the Blessed Eucharist, Love, are one and the same thing! In the Tabernacle we find the Host; in the Host, Jesus; in Jesus

His Heart; in His Heart, Love, Infinite Love, divine Charity, God, the Principle of life, living and vivifying. But more still; the ineffable miracle of the Eucharist can be explained only by love; by the love of God, yes, but by the love of Jesus, God and Man. Now the love of Jesus is the love of His Heart: it is His Heart, to sum up all in one word. Thus, the Blessed Eucharist is explained only by the Sacred Heart.

The Blessed Eucharist is the sublime completion of the love of Jesus for man. It is the highest, the last expression, the paroxysm, if one may so express it, of this incomprehensible love. Nevertheless, without the Eucharist we could have believed in love: the Incarnation would have been sufficient for that. A single drop of the cup of His bitter Passion would have been more than superabundant to prove to us this love. We would have been able to love the Heart of Jesus, we would have been bound to love It, to believe It sovereignly good, even if It had not gone to this divine excess of the Eucharist. But because He has invented this marvel how we should love this Sacred Heart, so divinely tender, so inexplicably delicate and liberal, and dare we say it, so madly inflamed with love for Its creature! Yes, the Blessed Eucharist augments, inflames our love for the divine Heart.

But because we know that we shall find this Sacred Heart only in the Blessed Eucharist; because we thirst for union with this Heart, so tender and so ardent, we go to the Blessed Eucharist, we prostrate ourselves before the Blessed Sacrament, we adore the divine Host radiating Its influence from the monstrance, we go to the holy Table with ardent avidity, we kiss lovingly the consecrated paten where the divine Host reposes each day. We surround with honor, respect, and magnificence the Tabernacle where Jesus, living and loving, makes His dwelling. Oh, it is impious to say that the worship of the Sacred Heart can injure Eucharistic worship. What? Will the knowledge of Him who gives, make us despise the gift? No, the more we love this divine Heart, the truer our worship to It is, the more extensive and enlightened it is, the more also our worship and love for the divine Eucharist will develop and grow strong.

VII

The Priest Another Jesus Christ

*T*HERE is in the bosom of God, an overflowing plenitude of love, which is His essence, His life, His movement, His fruitfulness. This plenitude has a continual need of pouring itself out, of flowing in a stream. It goes towards creation, towards man in particular, by a natural inclination. It is, as it were, a necessity for Love to fill the void of the creature and to give life to all things. Infinite Love is sometimes felt by the heart of man, but It is less known by his intellect. That is why so many shadows continue to lurk in the human intellect, especially in matters which regard the knowledge of God, of His mysteries and of supernatural truths.

For man, love should not be a mere sentiment which he experiences solely through the senses. It should be a knowledge received through his intellectual faculties. In the same measure in which a human soul comprehends Infinite Love by his mind and by his heart, it will also comprehend and enjoy the knowledge of the eternal truths and of all the mysteries of God. Infinite Love, like a divine fire, is heat for the heart of man, and light for his intellect. If man goes away from this hearth of love, his heart becomes cold, and his mind darkened.

Let us look at this sublime movement in God by which He attracts His beloved creature to Himself: it is a movement of love and mercy. He begins by taking hold of His priests to press them to His Heart, to bathe them in His love; then, through His priest, He takes hold of all souls.

Priests should therefore enter into a profound and constantly renewed knowledge of Infinite Love. The world cannot receive this revelation of love directly nor acquire for itself the fruits of grace and salvation that flow from it. It is the priest who, being nearer to God and already consecrated to Him, receives this manifestation of love, and who should communicate it to the world. By the Heart of Jesus, studied in the mystery of His divine virtues and imitated, the priest will enter into the full possession of the mystery of Infinite Love. He should not rest satisfied with receiving the devotion to the Heart of Jesus, with practicing it himself and communicating it to souls. That is very necessary without doubt; but Jesus wishes something different.

The priest should enter by the Sacred Heart into the intimate knowledge of Jesus Christ. It is like a door through which one must pass in order to penetrate into the interior of Christ, and, having become completely bathed and impregnated with Him, become like a brilliant mirror in which Infinite Love can be reflected.

Infinite Love is a sun. If it were to project its rays directly on the world, souls would be dazzled and consumed by it, because they are not sufficiently elevated or sufficiently pure. This divine Sun must be reflected in a mirror, and the reflection of its rays in this mirror will enlighten the world and warm it again. This mirror is the soul of the priest: but it must be pure, it must be transparent. The soul of the priest must become conformable to the soul of Christ. When the priest is truly another Jesus Christ, he becomes a very pure mirror capable of reflecting the divine radiation of Infinite Love

VIII

The Mystical Heart of Christ

*T*HE Heart of Christ manifests Itself to us, this time, not the Heart of flesh, meek and humble, pulsating in His human breast; not the sensible symbol of His ardent love, the sacred vessel in which the redeeming Blood was formed, and which the iron lance opened on Calvary; but the mystical Heart.

Has not Christ, the eternal Word of the Father, besides this Body of flesh which He has assumed in order to unite Himself better to our nature, a Mystical Body which He formed with Love, and of which He is the Head? And has not this Body like every living body, members and a heart? The Church is the Mystical Body of Christ, the faithful are its members, the Priesthood is its heart. Yes, the Priesthood is the heart of this living Body of which Christ is the Head!

A body dies if the head or the heart is mortally wounded, for it is from the head and the heart that life radiates through the entire body; but it can see many of its members fall off without the source of life drying up in it. Thus, the Church can at times see with sorrow some of its members perish, without its life failing; for its Head, Christ-Love, is immortal, and its Heart, its holy Priesthood grafted on Jesus, the eternal Priest, cannot perish.

According to the divine plan, the Priesthood, being the mystical heart of Christ and the true heart of the Church, is for the latter an organ of life as indispensable as the heart is for the human body. Without its Head, Christ, without its soul, the Holy Spirit, the Church would not exist; and without its heart, without its Priesthood which warms it and gives it life, it would be dead. It is by it that the divine movement which comes to it from its Head is communicated to all its members; that the life-giving blood of grace circulates even to its extremities; that the vital heat of love warms its members.

But what is the holy Priesthood in itself? It is a single organ, no doubt, but nevertheless composed of a multitude of parts. The Pontiffs, the priests, all the orders of the sacred hierarchy are its parts, its molecules, if we may so express it, which, united together, form the body of the Priesthood. The Priesthood is, then, what the parts which compose it are.

Now, the Priesthood is the heart of the Church, and in order that it perform in itself its operations of life, it must be robust and healthy; it must be free and ardent; its movement must be always full, always well balanced and always continuous.

I. *It must be robust and healthy.* It is its purity which makes it strong. The chaste priest is strong against himself, strong against the enemies who tempt him from within, and against those who attack him from without. By his purity he is raised above other men; he dominates them by his dignity and by the power which he acquires by the superhuman energy by which he conquers himself. By his purity he destroys the baneful germs which every man receives from his human descent, and if he cannot exterminate them completely, he renders them inactive.

II. *It must be free and ardent:* free from the obstructions which the hostility of the impious place in the way of the priest; free from human or ambitious views; free from seeking after sensual gratifications or human comfort; free from without, and free from within, with this true freedom which permits him to accomplish the work of Christ; but not with that false freedom demanded by certain independent, lawless spirits who trust only in themselves, and reject all legitimate authority.

III. *The movement of the heart of the Church should be full, always well balanced and always continuous.* If the priest leans on God for support, he cannot be shaken. In spite of the vicissitudes of earthly life, and in spite of his natural inconstancy, the faithful minister will accomplish the work of love without feebleness and without discouragement. He contributes his little share to vivify holy Church by the warmth of his zeal, by his active devotedness, by his ardent charity and especially by the gift of Jesus which he makes to souls.

IX

God Is Christ's, Christ Is the Priest's, the Priest Belongs to Souls

GOD is Christ's; Christ is the Priest's; and the Priest belongs to souls.

God is Christ's: Christ is God Himself. From the intimate possession which the humanity of Jesus has of the Divinity, and which the Divinity has of Jesus; from the sacred union, from the ineffable embrace of the two natures, Divine and human, which takes place in Jesus, there are born those marvellous charms of Christ; the greatness allied to profound humility, the justice allied to the most tender goodness, the strength united to unwearying patience, the sovereign sanctity joined to the most compassionate mercy. The brilliant rays of the Divinity of Christ, filtering through the transparent veil of His humanity, appear to us so radiant and sweet; and His humanity, transfigured by the divine light, seems to us so beautiful that every soul should hasten to Him and be united to this adorable marvel! Christ is the priest's! He has given Himself voluntarily to him. By the Blessed Eucharist, in the Holy Sacrifice, He becomes the divine possession of the priest. All Jesus: His spirit, His doctrine, His words, His most holy soul, His most loving Heart, His most pure Body, His Divinity, belong to the priest, who can dispose of these things as his goods, as his private possession. He takes Him in his hands, he slakes his thirst with His Blood; he nourishes himself with His Flesh; and not only does he live by Jesus, but he makes others live by Him. Not only can he enjoy the possession of Jesus, but He can give Him to other souls, and make them also enjoy Him.

Christ is the priest's. The priest is also Christ's. There must be reciprocity. And because Christ has given Himself entirely to the priest, in like manner the priest should belong entirely to Jesus. Entirely: his mind, his heart, his body; that is to say his whole intellect, all his thoughts, all his affections and his wishes, all his works, all the movements of his life.

The priest is Christ's. Christ can then dispose of him with the same power as the priest disposes of Jesus. In order that there may be equality, the priest, in the hands of Christ, should be such as the white Host is in the hands of the priest. Let us meditate on the divine profundity of this union of Christ with the priest and of the priest with Christ. It is not like the union of the Word with the Humanity in Jesus, but it is, nevertheless, something very close and very intimate.

The priest belongs to souls! He is their possession, as he is the possession of Christ. He belongs to them; he no longer belongs to himself, he can no longer live for himself. He must be completely given, completely consecrated to souls. Does not the mother belong to her child? Ought she not to give him all he needs, and has he not the right to all the helps which she can give him in his weakness? And the child also belongs to the mother. He is her property; he is a deposit that God has entrusted to her. She carries him about wherever she wishes. She caresses him or rebukes him; she disposes of him as she wishes for his good, and has the right to obedience from him. In like manner, souls belong to the priest; and from this double possession, effected in the spirit and in the grace of Jesus, there should arise on the part of the priest unbounded devotedness; on the part of souls, confidence without reserve.

Let us consider all the exquisite delicacy that should exist in the heart of the priest for the souls that have become his goods, his splendid possession in Christ; and the respect and confidence that should exist in souls for the priest whom God has given to them to conduct them to Him.

Oh, what grand things God has done! What marvels His Infinite Love has performed! But how feeble and dim are the eyes of man! How poor his intellect! There is, in all this, reason to make us go into an ecstasy of love, but the load of our human misery weighs us down too heavily!

X

The Dispenser of Infinite Love

*T*HE priest has been made the dispenser of the mysteries of God (*1 Cor.* 4:1), and of the treasures of His love. All these things have been placed in his hands in order that he may distribute them to souls. He has in himself, so to speak, the deposit of the mysteries of uncreated Truth, and of the treasures of Infinite Love. Oh, how great the priest is, and how worthy of respect and honor!

But if he is a dispenser, he ought to dispense. Each soul should receive from him all that is necessary for his intellect and his heart. God gives some graces directly to souls, as the rich man gives an alms to the poor whom he happens to meet. But He wishes that the greatest part of

His graces to be distributed go to souls by the hands of the priest, like the rich man who has the larger alms distributed by the steward that he has chosen.

The priest, then, has in his possession, not to keep, but to distribute, all the treasures of Truth and Love. If he does not give these divine, living gifts, he holds them back, he hoards them unjustly, he deprives souls of them, and he renders himself blameworthy. On the contrary, if he distributes them, he is a faithful and blessed dispenser. He is more than that still; he is a living and vivifying channel by which Infinite Love makes Its sacred streams pass.

XI

The Intermediary Between God and Man

ALL human creatures may approach God personally with confidence, for God is the Creator of all, the Father of all, He loves them all. The Incarnate Word, Christ-Love, is the divine Person who introduces souls into the presence of the Father, and by Him, they are certain of being lovingly welcomed. Nevertheless, our great God wishes, our adorable Jesus wishes, that in a great number of circumstances, His humble creature, in order to approach Him, make use of the intermediary whom He Himself has designated to present to Him souls and the sacrifices and gifts which they wish to offer to Him. This intermediary chosen by God is the Priest.

God, in His wisdom and love, has formed a sort of mysterious ladder or chain which goes from the creature to the Divinity: the material creature to man, man to the priest, the priest to Christ and Christ to God. And from Infinite Love, from God Himself, all gifts and graces descend by this same chain of love even to the humblest and last of creatures: God, Infinite Love, to Christ, Christ to the priest, the priest to the multitude of men, men to the material creation. Infinite Love, thus passes and repasses in perpetual flow from God to His creation, and from His creation to God.

XII

The Blessed Virgin and the Priest

*T*HE love of the priest for Jesus should be different from the love of other men for Him and singularly more ardent, for, "He who has received more, loves more." (*Luke* 7:42–47). Now, the graces and particular gifts which enrich the soul and heart of the priest are in such great number that he who has received them and possesses them is not even conscious of all he has received, and even when he is aware that he has received much, he cannot know all the profuseness of grace which Infinite Love has lavished on him. It will be one of the enjoyments of the priest in Heaven to see and to know all that Love has done for him, and how privileged he has been among other men.

The priest, in a certain manner, passes to the state of being divinized by the union which he has with Christ, and by the power which, through Christ, he has over souls for their good and for their salvation. Thus he is bound to have for God, Our Lord, a love particularly strong, tender, and ardent.

There is only one creature who has loved, and who loves Jesus as the priest should love Him; there is only one heart which can serve as a model to him for this love; it is the heart of the Most Holy Virgin. The love of the priest for Jesus should be in everything like the love of Mary for her divine Son.

Like Mary, the priest, elevated to a very high degree by a grace of preference, nevertheless remains an inferior creature, in submission to the divine Master. Like her, he touches on nothingness by his nature, and on intimacy with the divinity, by a privilege of love. Like her, he should be more enlightened on the truth of his own misery and wretchedness, and more influenced by divine radiations of Infinite Love. Like her, he receives from the Omnipotence of the Holy Ghost the power to produce the Word Incarnate in the world: the Mother produces Him in the truth of His visible flesh; the priest in the truth of His Eucharistic Flesh.

The love of Mary for Jesus is a love of a privileged creature. It is a love of ardent gratitude and profound humility; a love which abases itself and devotes itself; which gives itself entirely by the necessity of returning all possible to Him from whom all has been received. The love of Mary is also a love of a mother; tender, delicate, eager love; a love which defends and protects, which sacrifices itself again, but in a different manner, which gives itself, not to make a return, but to give again to Him to whom she has already given.

The love of the priest for Jesus, his adorable Master, should be altogether similar. He should have a love of humble gratitude, a love of a loved creature who adores, who thanks, who gives himself without counting; a love full of exquisite delicacy; a jealous love which guards with vigilance, which protects, which surrounds with loving attentions, a love of one who sacrifices himself even to utter forgetfulness of self.

Mary had for Jesus not only the love of a privileged creature and of a loving mother; she had, in addition, she has always for her adorable Son the love of a virgin. It is a humble love too; love ought to be always humble; but a confiding love, faithful, unique, full of chaste familiarities and respectful ardor.

Such should also be the love of the priest for Jesus; a pure love, a love free from entanglement, faithful and confiding. The priest has not, it is true, the ideal whiteness of the Immaculate. His heart has not the sublime purity of that of the Virgin Mother. But he has only to draw from the graces of his priesthood; he will find there sources of virginal tenderness and heroic devotedness.

Jesus wishes to be loved by His priests as He has been loved by the Virgin Mary, and He has included in the privilege of the priesthood graces similar to those contained in the privilege of the divine Maternity: graces of intimate and altogether singular union with

His adorable Person; graces of ineffable purity; graces of unreserved devotedness.

XIII

"Feed My Sheep"

O NE day Our Lord said to Peter: "Feed My lambs. . . . Feed My sheep." (*John* 21:15 etc.). According to the common interpretation, the lambs are the faithful; the sheep, the pastors; and is not the priest the pastor of the flock confided to him? In this single word, "sheep," Jesus has included, in abbreviated form, all the duties of the priest: his duties towards God, towards the Roman Pontiff, the Vicar of Jesus Christ, towards his brethren in the priesthood, towards souls.

The sheep belongs entirely to its master: it owes to him its life, its fertility; he has a right to dispose of it as he wishes. The priest belongs entirely to God, his sovereign Master. He belongs entirely to Jesus Christ; he owes Him the fertility of his works, and if need be, the sacrifice of his life. The sheep should be docile to the pastor who directs it in the name of the master. It should answer his voice; it should follow him to the pasture where he conducts it, and be obedient and faithful. In the same manner the priest should be obedient to the voice of the supreme Pastor; he should enter into His views, nourish his soul only on the doctrines which He approves of, and remain faithful and unshakably submissive to the pastoral staff of Peter.

Each sheep of the flock has no other duties towards those around it but meekness and union. It must not go away from the flock or remain alone, for it would expose itself to perish. Jesus wishes His priests to have a close bond of union among themselves; He wishes that they guard the unity of the Faith in the bond of fraternal charity, and that, working in the same spirit, they give peace to the world and glory to God.

Finally the sheep is a mother, a mother of lambs. She carries them in her womb, she nourishes them with her milk, she warms them and she guards them. The priest is not only a father of souls: he is their mother also. He should have for them the tender and delicate love of mothers, their devotedness, even to self-sacrifice. He ought to give to souls the best of his own substance, the substance of a soul that is spiritual and very pure; he ought to warm them with the flames of Infinite Love and guard them from evil.

We find in these considerations an adorable mark of the divinity of the Saviour. Man requires many words to express an idea; Jesus, by a single word, gives a whole, harmonious collection of thoughts. This is seen at each step in the Holy Gospels. By this one word 'sheep,' thrown out in conversation as if by chance, Jesus says everything about the priest; all that he ought to be, all that he ought to do, all that he ought to give of himself to God, to the Church, to souls. Ah! it is because Jesus is the Word. He is the divine thought and the uncreated Word. A single word fallen from His lips contains a thought of God.

How good it is to know Jesus, so grand in His divinity, so sweet in His humanity! Would that it were given to us to be able to express the little we know of Him, to make Him known, to make Him loved, to gain for Him adoration, to surround Him with praises, with love, with glory, and to exalt Him to infinity.

XIV

Love and Justice

GOD *is too good, He cannot punish eternally.* It is thus that many judge Thee, O Lord. And under this vain pretext, they prefer to serve their passions and their evil inclinations, rather than renounce themselves and follow Thee, O Jesus.

Nothing, however is more contrary to the doctrine of the Church: Hell is far from being opposed to Thy goodness, and it is precisely because I believe in Thy love, O my great God, powerful and good, that I believe in Hell.

If Thou were not Love; if, egoistically shut up in Thy happiness, Thou didst cast on beings inferior to Thyself only indifferent looks, perhaps Hell might not exist. But Thou! Thou hast created everything through love. Thou hast formed man to Thy divine image; Thou hast vivified him by Thy own breath; Thou hast filled him with Thy gifts, and Thou hast demanded from this creature so richly endowed only a little confidence, a little fidelity and love. And when he despises Thee and revolts against Thee, wouldst Thou remain impassible, like an incomplete Being devoid of love and feeling? O my God, I believe in the rigors of Thy justice, because I believe in the excessive tenderness of Thy Heart!

I love Thee, my God, Infinite Love, who dost bend down towards Thy creature, who dost sustain him and raise him up. But I love Thee also, disowned and outraged Love, who dost vindicate Thyself and punish. If Hell did not exist, I would not love Thee so much. When I see a prince allow all crimes to go unpunished in his kingdom; when I see his largess distributed with equal profusion to felons and traitors as to loyal subjects, and see the royal greatness and majesty dragged in the mire, I cannot but despise him and call him unjust and cowardly. No, if there were no Hell I could not love Thee . . . If there were no Hell three splendid jewels would be wanting to the crown of Thy sublime perfections; there would be wanting justice, power and dignity!

I love Thee, I adore Thee, my God, in Thy mercy for the weak, in Thy goodness towards the little ones, in Thy liberality towards the poor. I adore Thee in Thy pardons without reserve, in that ineffable love which descends from Thy bosom to Thy creatures; in Thy unwearied patience to sinners; in fine, in these graces which Thou dost pour forth in profusion on souls to touch them, to bring them back, to enlighten them, to conquer them!

I adore Thee also, I love Thee passionately, Thou great, majestic, terrible God, consuming in eternal flames those who have resisted the embraces of Thy love.

And besides, it is not Thee, my God sovereignly good, who dost condemn and damn; it is those wicked people themselves who, refusing to throw themselves into the flames of Thy eternal love, precipitate themselves into those of Thy eternal Justice! Yes, I love Thee such as Thou art. I adore Thee, crowned with the infinite collection of all perfections, as just as Thou art good, as great by Thy power and by Thy holiness, as by Thy mercy, and always Love, Infinite Love; Love which creates, which gives, which pardons, which vivifies; Love which commands, which corrects, and which chastises![7]

---

7. For Examination to be made each day, and Act of Consecration and Donation to Infinite Love see pages 183, 184.

APPENDIX

Foundation of "The Priests' Universal Union of the Friends of the Sacred Heart"

*D*URING these long years of waiting for the realization of the first part of her work, many things happened to Mother Louise Margaret in which we can now recognize the Hand of Providence aiding her in carrying out her mission.

The Community to which she belonged was expelled from France during the religious persecution. After weary journeys through many parts of Europe, in which Sister Louise Margaret accompanied the Rev. Mother, a place of refuge was at last found for the Community in the diocese of Ivrea near Turin, under Monsignor Filipello in 1906. The following year Mother Louise Margaret was elected Rev. Mother, a position which she occupied for the canonical term of six years.

It was this Monsignor Filipello who aided her in the publication of *The Sacred Heart and the Priesthood,* and as has been already mentioned, it was he who presented the book to His Holiness Pope Pius X. When the book was published, he asked Mother Louise for further details about the origin of the book and the end that it was intended to serve. In reply, she sent him all her manuscripts for examination, and on October 10th, 1910, wrote him the following letter:

"As I think I have already told Your Excellency, for several years the interior lights which I received in prayer had reference to the infinite love of God, or rather to Infinite Love, God Himself, and I felt that these lights and these teachings were not given for myself alone. . . . It was at the end of 1902 that the idea of an organization for priests was communicated to me. I had always faithfully handed over my papers to Father Charrier, and in 1904 he seemed decided to undertake something according to the desires of Jesus, but seized with fear at the sight of his unworthiness . . . he did not dare to go forward . . . I pressed him respectfully, because Our Saviour urged me interiorly, but time and courage were always wanting in him."

"In March, 1909, it seemed to me that Our Saviour made known His complaints that nothing had been done. In fact nearly seven years had elapsed since the demands were made by Jesus. I transmitted these demands to Father Charrier, and feeling myself powerless to respond to the desires of Our Saviour, I wrote a letter to the Sovereign Pontiff. . . . It seems to me that Jesus wishes an organization that will unite priests—the good and faithful ones—around their bishop in each diocese, and that these dioceses be linked together and grouped around the Pope. . . .

"The priests of this organization (which will not be merely a work of prayer, like that of Father Eymard, but an active work) will labor in the spirit of the little book—*The Sacred Heart and the Priesthood*—to spread the knowledge of Infinite Love around them and preach love for Jesus Christ, God and man, and fidelity to the Church and the Pope. As for the exterior organization of this work, it seems to me that the person whom Our Lord will call to found it will know, better than I, the most suitable way to establish it."

Having examined her manuscripts, Monsignor Filipello wrote to her asking her to make out a draft for the statutes of the proposed Priests' Universal Union so as to give the work a concrete form. In a subsequent letter he asked her to write out for him all the passages in her writings that had reference to this work, and to draw up an appeal to priests. Mother Louise Margaret obeyed.

By March, 1911, she had completed the draft-copy of the statutes and the appeal to priests and sent them to His Excellency.

He visited Rome in the following May, where he presented the draft-copy of the Statutes and the "Appeal to Priests" first to Cardinal Gennari, and afterwards to Pope Pius X. Both the Cardinal and the Holy Father encouraged Monsignor Filipello to go on with the work, but the Holy Father decided that he should wait some time so that this Universal Organization should not be confounded with another local sacerdotal organization that was then being formed.

Monsignor Filipello waited two years. During this time Mother Louise received further lights on the work, which she communicated to him, and at his request revised the Statutes, giving them their present form. In March, 1913, Monsignor Filipello gave them his official approbation under the title: "Statutes of the Priests' Universal Union of the Friends of the Sacred Heart."[8]

---

8.   For Statutes see page 181.

This was only the official approbation of the Statutes of the new association. Owing to many circumstances, among which was the outbreak of the World War in 1914, seven years were yet to elapse before the first branch could be formed. During this period, a series of Providential events brought Mother Louise Margaret to Rome. In May, 1913, her second term as Superioress came to an end, and she was relieved of her charge. It was her own wish to efface herself completely, and live as the least member of the community, but she found it impossible to carry out her wishes in practice after the profound personal influence which she had exercised during her two terms of office. The extraordinary confessor advised that she be sent to another convent of the Order, and the new Superioress was of the same opinion.

Monsignor Filipello was most reluctant that she should leave his diocese, but when he learned that she was being sent to the Visitation Convent in Rome, he willingly gave his consent, hoping that her presence there would help to forward the work of the Priests' Universal Union.

He therefore ordered her to proceed to Rome, and entrusted her with the final draft of the Statutes to be presented to the Holy See. He gave her a letter of introduction to Cardinal Genarri, Prefect of the Congregation of the Council, and instructed her to have the lights which she had received in prayer examined by competent authority at Rome.

On her way to Rome she passed by Bologna, where Cardinal Della Chiesa, the future Pope Benedict XV, was then Archbishop. Contradictory orders as to where she should go, which she had just received, made it necessary for her to acquaint His Eminence with the circumstances of her case. He ordered her to continue her journey to Rome. *It was he who later on as Pope protected the new order of nuns founded by her, even providing for its material wants, and acted as a father to the new community after her early death.*

When she arrived at Rome, she presented Monsignor Filipello's letter to Cardinal Genarri and the draft-copy of the Statutes, and, as directed, handed in all her manuscripts for examination. Monsignor Filipello's approbation of the Statutes was confirmed at Rome. Mother Louise Margaret sent them to him with the following letter:

"Monsignor Galardo returned me these Statutes which I enclose for Your Excellency. He has found nothing to be changed or corrected . . . . He believes that the organization of the Priests' Universal Union will give general satisfaction, being clear and simple, and easy to accommodate to all places and circumstances, and especially because it provides a bond of charity . . . . "

While she was at Rome, the communications which she believed she received from Our Lord about the foundation of a convent of Nuns to cooperate with the priests of the Priests' Universal Union was inquired into. The decision of the Holy See was that it was the will of God that such a foundation should be made, and she was entrusted with the task.

When her business in Rome was concluded, she was sent back to Monsignor Filipello who had given permission to have this new Monastery of the Visitation founded in his diocese. This house was formally opened on March 25th, 1914. Mother Louise Margaret died in May of the following year.

Many questions about the new foundation remained to be settled after the early death of the foundress. These were finally settled at Rome under Benedict XV, in 1918, and about the same time the World War came to an end. In the same year Monsignor Filipello proceeded with the formation of the first branch of the Priests' Universal Union. Two years later, in October, 1920, nine priests pronounced their act of consecration and donation to Infinite Love before the Blessed Sacrament exposed, in the chapel of Bethany of the Sacred Heart, the newly-founded convent.

The manner in which the work was to develop, small and humble in the beginning like the early Church with the vitality of the mustard-seed, and the need for a bond of union between the priests of the world, are indicated in the following quotations from lights which Mother Louise Margaret received in prayer:

"There is question of choosing some priests marked by God to be the first to receive the revelation of Love . . . . and they will communicate the divine fire to their brethren, and thus Infinite Love will do Its work, and make Its progress like a fire which breaks out in the corner of a forest and gradually spreads to all the trees, causing a general conflagration." (July, 1912).

December, 1912. "It seems to me that Jesus wishes to form a bond of union between His Sacred Heart and all the elite of His priests. There are many excellent sacerdotal organizations, but none that is general and universal . . . because each country and each province has its particular needs, and the organizations created correspond to these needs.

"Nevertheless, if I am not deceived, Jesus wishes something universal, something catholic, which will unite by a very simple and very strong bond all the other organizations already formed."

The Founding of the New Sisterhood, called "Bethany of the Sacred Heart" and of "The Faithful Friends of Bethany of the Sacred Heart"

*S*ISTERS as well as priests, men and women living in the world as well as Religious, were to be called on to cooperate in the work of rekindling the flame of divine love in a world grown cold and turning away from God. As early as 1899, Mother Louise Margaret had received lights on the foundation of the new convent and a vision of the actual house in Italy in which the new religious community afterwards found a home. On her way to Rome, two Superiors of convents through which she passed had, of their own initiative, advised her to make a new foundation. At Rome, Cardinal Gennari, Prefect of the Congregation of the Council, and Cardinal Cagiano, Prefect of the Congregation for Religious, not only advised her to make a new foundation, but told her that such was the will of God in her regard. They favored an order in which the Sisters would devote themselves to a life of prayer and self-immolation for priests.

On the advice of the Cardinal Prefect of the Congregation for Religious, she drew up a formal petition for the foundation of a new convent, and received the approbation of the Sacred Congregation. Monsignor Filipello invited her to found the new Convent in his diocese. Having concluded all her business at Rome, she was invited to an audience with Pope Pius X and having received encouragement and a special blessing from His Holiness, she departed for Turin where Monsignor Filipello had arranged that the Sisters of Charity should give her hospitality until she should find a suitable house for the new foundation.

A house at Vische near Turin was offered to them. The proprietor had wished that the house should be acquired by a religious community, and so, arrangements for leasing the house were quickly made with goodwill. The daughter of the proprietor, Miss Louise Rossi, tells as follows the story of how the house was leased:

"My mother had many times expressed the desire that one of our houses that enshrines sacred memories should be inhabited by religious. On a certain rainy day, a Saturday, a day dedicated to the Blessed Virgin, my mother, urged by a secret inspiration, went to the Bishop of Ivrea on this business and told him of her intentions. Now while she was at the Bishop's house, Sister Margaret, the worthy companion of Mother Louise Margaret, happened to be there also. The Sisters were looking for a house; my mother was in search of Religious to live in one of her houses. In presence of this happy coincidence, Monsignor Filipello exclaimed: 'This is truly providential!' "

The new foundation began with three professed Sisters of the Visitation and one postulant. It was begun without any monetary resources, but Providence furnished what was necessary; and as it was the will of Providence that the little community should imitate the poverty of Bethlehem, the Sisters lived in the greatest want, having what was barely sufficient for each day.

This community has at present fifty Sisters at the Mother-house at Vische, Turin, and eleven at a branch convent recently founded at Orleans. They have besides applications from several other countries to found branches.

They are a contemplative order. They offer up their lives and all their works for the welfare of the Pope, bishops, and priests of the Church. Eight hours of their day is spent in prayer, which includes the recitation of the Divine Office the same as priests. The rest of their day is spent in manual labor. Thus founded as they have been in poverty, and living by the labor of their hands, they reproduce the life of the Holy Family at Nazareth.

"The Associates of the Priests' Universal Union" and "The Faithful Friends of Bethany of the Sacred Heart"

*B*ISHOPS and priests were to be the first recipients of the new message of love, so that they might communicate it to the world by means of the new sacerdotal organization: a special Sisterhood was to cooperate with the new organization and have that as their *raison d'etre.* But the rest of the faithful both religious and laity were also called upon to cooperate in the regeneration of the world. That also was part of the message of Mother Louise Margaret.

In September, 1914, she wrote to Father Charrier: "The will of God seems to me to be that we unite to our little community souls from the world who have an attraction for Infinite Love, and for praying for priests. For myself, I think that the book to give inspiration for the exterior life is: *The Introduction to the Devout Life* by St. Francis de Sales, and that the impulse towards the interior life should be taken from the knowledge of Infinite Love and from the act of consecration to Infinite Love; and that the end should be to pray for the Church and the Priesthood."

The ecclesiastical authorities have carried out this wish of Mother Louise Margaret and have founded two other branches, one for men and the other for women, membership in which is open to all, both lay and religious, other than priests and Sisters of Bethany of the Sacred Heart.

The branch for men is called "The Associates of the Priests' Universal Union" and is composed of Brothers, whether belonging to Orders devoted to teaching or works of mercy, or lay-brothers of Religious Orders, and of laymen.

The branch for women is called "The Faithful Friends of Bethany of the Sacred Heart" and is composed of Sisters of all Religious Orders other than those of Bethany of the Sacred Heart, and women living in the world.

This cooperation of all the faithful, both religious and lay, with the bishops and priests, to enkindle the fire of divine love again in a world that is turning away from God, is in accordance with the spirit of Catholic Action, and will certainly prove a God-sent help to Catholic Action, imparting to that movement new spiritual vigor, and helping to unify its activity.

The divine plan for these two auxiliary branches is the same as that for the principal ones; to fill the members themselves with the love of God so that they would act as channels to communicate it to the world. The Statutes of the Priests' Universal Union, except those parts which have reference to priests alone, constitute the rule of life both for the personal sanctification of the members and their external apostolate. A glance at those Statutes given below will show that the cooperation asked for from religious and laity imposes no burden that cannot be easily borne by anyone of goodwill. The extent of cooperation is left to each one's zeal.

As might be expected, Religious have taken the lead in the work of these two auxiliary organizations. Not only have individual Religious from various Orders become zealous members of the Associates of the Priests' Universal Union and of the Faithful Friends of Bethany, but whole communities of Religious have joined the Associates of the Priests' Universal Union and of Bethany of the Sacred Heart.

Priests of Religious Orders and the Priests' Universal Union

*T*HE principal object of this Association is to unite the priests around their bishops, and the bishops and priests of the world around the Pope in the work of making known the doctrine of Infinite Love. The control of the diocesan branches, then, is to be in the hands of the bishop or one of the priests of his diocese. With regard to priests of Religious Orders, the Statutes read as follows: "Although this work is specially intended for priests of the secular clergy, priests of Religious Orders can become members, individually, on the same conditions of admission."

In two letters to Monsignor Filipello, Mother Louise Margaret expresses her wishes as to how priests of Religious Orders are to help this Work. In June, 1911, she writes: "Our Lord addresses His Work of Love to His priests; His object is to bring the secular clergy more closely together and unite them around their bishop. Priests of Religious Orders can nourish themselves on the doctrine of Infinite Love, become penetrated with it, consecrate themselves to Infinite Love and preach it everywhere . . . . It would be very desirable that the diocesan Directors and Presidents of Conferences should invite priests of Religious Orders to preach at their meetings."

In July, 1913, she wrote: "On Friday, while I was before the Blessed Sacrament, Our Lord made known to me several things about His priests. He wishes that we should work to uplift them not only in the esteem of the world, but also in their own esteem, in order that they may become more and more attached to their sublime vocation. Jesus makes no difference in His Heart between secular priests and priests of Religious Orders. He said that there were people who wished to create an order of men suited to the needs of our time, but that the true Apostles of our present time should be all priests without distinction and especially the secular clergy. The Bishops and priests form the order *par excellence* of our epoch."

The Priests' Universal Union and Other Associations for Priests

RELATIONS with other Clerical Associations.

The Priests' Universal Union has an aim, an object and a work to do different from all other existing Associations. The aim of the Union has been defined by Mother Louise Margaret as follows: "This Union which we call The Priests' Universal Union of the *Friends* of the Sacred Heart—in order to honor the saying of Jesus Christ to His Apostles: 'I will not now call you servants; for the servant knoweth not what his Lord doth, but I have called you *friends*'" (*John* 15:15)—has as its end: a) to group together all the priests of the world around the Adorable Heart of Our Saviour Jesus Christ, in order to array them as an elite body against the errors and corruption of our time; b) to restore and develop the family spirit and the spirit of solidarity in the sacerdotal body, to make the same spirit circulate through it and to establish in it a more complete unity of views, a more uniform movement of action;

c) to procure the personal sanctification of its members by a true and practical devotion to Our Lord Jesus Christ and His Sacred Heart, the Tabernacle of Infinite Love, and to procure the sanctification of souls in general by the development and good direction of the Apostolic spirit."

It is therefore in no sense a rival, and in no way interferes with the work of other clerical Unions. On the contrary, it aims at assisting them and, so far from trying to take members away from them, its work will result in increasing their numbers. Members of other clerical Unions who join will still remain members of these unions and will be expected to become more zealous members; clerical associations which become affiliated will retain their identity and will receive valuable help. The Priests' Universal Union of the Friends of the Sacred Heart has much to offer. It provides priests of other societies with books specially suited for priests, which the Holy See has examined and has allowed to be published as private revelation containing a message from Our Lord to priests and directions for their priestly life and apostolic labors. It promotes unity and harmony between the members of the various clerical associations and between the members themselves, its motto being the prayer of Our Lord at the Last Supper for His Apostles: "That they be one as We also are One." (*John* 18:22).

The following quotations from the letters of Mother Louise Margaret show 1) the need for the Priests' Universal Union; 2) that it does not aim at supplanting other clerical associations; and 3) that it will help them by infusing new life and vigor without adding any heavy burden.

"It seems to me that Jesus wishes an organization which will unite the good and faithful priests and group them around their bishops in each diocese, and that these dioceses be linked together and grouped around the Pope."

(Letter to Monsignor Filipello, Oct., 1910)

"For the past two or three years, and even this year, associations for priests have been formed in different dioceses; that makes for much diversity without however effecting the unity which Jesus demanded and still demands."

(Letter to Father Charrier, June, 1911)

"Indeed this Work of Love (The Priests' Universal Union), so long desired and demanded by the Divine Master, seems to me to consist in a universal bond between priests based on the love which Jesus has for them, and which they ought to have for Jesus. This must necessarily begin in some diocese, but it must not be a diocesan work. It is something universal that Jesus wishes, something that can be accommodated to all places, all minds and all usages."

(Letter to Father Charrier, June, 1911)

"Our Lord asks very specially of priests, obedience of spirit, dependence on the guidance of their bishops, love for Himself, the Divine Priest and love for souls that are so dear to Him."

(*Letter to Monsignor Filipello*, February, 1918)

"I have shown the Work (the Priests' Universal Union) as a bond of universal charity destined to be, not indeed an extra work added to the other works which are already numerous, but an all-embracing bond uniting together all other associations and making complete fusion of all the priests of the world together."

(*Letter from Rome to Monsignor Filipello*, December, 1913)

Other sacerdotal associations can be affiliated (even if these associations are not formed for purely spiritual ends), provided they be willing to adopt the spirit of the Priests' Universal Union.

The sacerdotal associations which become affiliated to the Priests' Universal Union do not thereby become dependent on it or come under its authority, but form a simple bond of charity and cooperation—in other words they form a purely spiritual bond.

Clerical associations which become affiliated to the Priests' Universal Union, should take their inspiration for their activities, even material, from the doctrine of Infinite Love, which is essentially a doctrine of charity.

A person who is a member of an association which is affiliated to the Priests' Universal Union does not thereby become a member of that Union. If he wishes to become a member, he must join in the ordinary way.

The Priests' Universal Union, then, does not aim at supplanting any other associations actually existing, but at infusing new spirit into them, the spirit of love of God and fraternal charity, drawn from Infinite Love in the Sacred Heart of Jesus. In fact it aims at helping other works already existing to expand and unite, without losing their individual character and object, and to work for the reign of Infinite Love in the world.

Thus, great Sacerdotal Associations among which, the Apostolic Union of Secular Priests of the Sacred Heart, the Society of Priests of St. Francis de Sales and the Priest Apostles of the Sacred Heart of Mont Martre, have been affiliated to the Priests' Universal Union. In the same manner entire communities of Sisters have been affiliated to the Institute of Bethany of the Sacred Heart by a spiritual bond of prayer and charity. Thus gradually the promise of Our Lord to Mother Louise Margaret is being realized: "It is you who are to bring the overflow of My Infinite Love to all priests and through them to the extremities of the world."

The Book of Infinite Love

As HAS been already mentioned, Mother Louise Margaret had been using the term "Infinite Love," for God, all through her writings; her "Intimate Notes" are full of lights on the Unity and Trinity of God under the aspect of Infinite Love; besides, the principal object of the Priests' Universal Union and of the Societies allied to it, is to preach Infinite Love, and so Monsignor Filipello and others urged her to write a little book on Infinite Love in which she would put those lights into the form of a treatise, as she had done so beautifully for those which she had received on the Priesthood.

It was only under obedience to the Bishop's authority and with the greatest diffidence that she undertook such a difficult work. She devoted to it all the spare time of the last few years of her life. As usual, she submitted the plan of the work to Father Charrier, who was already in possession of all the revelations which she received on the subject. In his reply to her he wrote: "This adorable name of God which is revealed in a definite way only in St. John's: 'Deus est Caritas' (*1 John* 4:8); God is Infinite Love; the manner in which you express this striking truth, and all that I have read in your papers (the intimate notes which were to serve for the composition of the book on Infinite Love), prove that Our Lord is guiding your pen with a sublime simplicity which is the seal of divine assistance. Your plan pleased me very much. . . . Yes, speak of Infinite Love since Our Lord reveals it to you. . . ."

She was taken seriously ill before she had time to complete the work but not before she had written the most important part of it and had left the plan and the material for the rest. The work was completed after her death by inserting quotations from her 'Intimate Notes' into the plan which she left.

When the public devotion to the Sacred Heart was being given to the world as the great means to bring it back to fervor, while St. Margaret Mary Alacoque was appointed by Our Lord as the Apostle of that work, several other holy souls, both before and after her time, were favored with similar visions of the Sacred Heart and similar revelations of the greatness of Its love for men. Indeed, the revelations made to St. Gertrude and St. Matilda agree almost verbatim with those made to St. Margaret Mary.

In modern times, a new message of love is conveyed to priests, and through them to the world, through Mother Louise Margaret. At the same time Our Lord uses other holy souls to convey that same message.

What is practically a summary of the books of Mother Louise Margaret will be found in the great Encyclical of His Holiness Pius X to the bishops and priests of the world, which was issued in 1908.

A book called *Christ's Appeal to Love*[9] was published in 1938 with a letter of recommendation by His present Holiness Pius XII when he was Cardinal Pacelli. It contains the communications received by a Sister Josefa Menendez of the Society of the Sacred Heart of Jesus, who was a contemporary of Mother Louise Margaret.

The following quotation from this book shows a remarkable similarity between the message conveyed by Sister Josefa Menendez and that of Mother Louise Margaret:

"And now lastly I address Myself to My Own consecrated ones, that they may make Me known to sinners and to the world.

"Many are as yet unable to understand what My true feelings are. They treat Me as One from Whom they live apart, know only slightly, and in Whom they have little confidence. Let them rekindle their faith and love and live trustfully in My intimacy, loving and loved.

"It is usually the eldest son of the family who best knows the secrets and feelings of his father. In him the father is wont to confide more than in the younger ones, who as yet are unable to interest themselves in serious matters, or penetrate deeper than the surface. So when the father comes to die, it behoves the elder brother to transmit his wishes and will to these his younger brethren.

"In My Church I, too, have elder sons: They are those whom I Myself have chosen; consecrated by the priesthood or by the vows of religion. They are those who live nearest to Me; they share in My choicest graces, and to them I confide My secrets. Through their ministry they have charge of their brothers, My little children, and to them is entrusted either directly or indirectly the care of instructing and guiding them and of transmitting to them My Will.

"If those chosen souls truly know Me, they will be able to make Me known to others; if they love Me, they will be able to make Me loved; but how can they teach others when they hardly know Me themselves? Is there much love in one's heart for Him Whom one does not know? Or what intimate converse is possible with One from Whom association is cut off? What trust, what little confidence is felt?

"This is precisely what I wish to recall to the minds of My chosen ones; it is nothing new, no doubt, but have they no need to reanimate their faith, their love and trust?"

If anyone finds it difficult to believe that in our own day Our Lord should speak again from the Tabernacle to chosen souls who have shared in His suffering life, the answer given by Father Galliffet, S.J., who was a contemporary of St. Margaret Mary, to those who had similar difficulties about the favors

---

9.   An English translation of this book can be had from all Catholic booksellers.

which she received, might help to solve his doubts. It is as follows:

"These favors seem extraordinary, but if it should appear to any Catholic strange or extraordinary that Our Saviour should give His Heart to St. Gertrude or to St. Margaret Mary, is it not more extraordinary that He should give His Body and Blood to ordinary sinful mortals?

"If we had not this doctrine and reality of the Mass and the Blessed Eucharist and the real presence in the Tabernacle, and if we were told that Our Saviour, for some privileged soul, should put Himself under the appearance of bread, to give that privileged person His Body and Blood; and that, to console that person He should consent to remain always near at hand under these species, would it not seem incredible? So we are not to measure with our feeble minds the infinite love of Christ."

Statutes of the Priests' Universal Union of the Friends of the Sacred Heart

I. END OF THE WORK. This work which we call "The Priests' Universal Union of the Friends of the Sacred Heart" in order to honor this saying of Jesus Christ to His Apostles: "I will not now call you servants; for the servant knoweth not what his Lord doth, but I have called you friends" (*John* 15:15), has as its end: a) to group together all the priests of the world around the adorable Heart of Our Saviour Jesus Christ in order to array them as an elite body against the errors and corruption of our time; b) to restore and develop the family spirit, and the spirit of solidarity in the Sacerdotal Body, to make the same spirit circulate through it and to establish in it a more complete unity of views, a more uniform movement of action; c) to procure the personal sanctification of its members by a true and practical devotion to Our Lord Jesus Christ and His Sacred Heart, the tabernacle of Infinite Love, and to procure the sanctification of souls in general, by the development and the good direction of the Apostolic spirit.

II. SPIRIT OF THE WORK. Urged by the sublime impulse given by Pius X the priests who form part of this Union undertake, under the guidance of their bishops and the direction of the Holy See, "to restore all things in Christ."

By their word, by their works, by their writing, especially by their example and their lives entirely modelled on that of Jesus Christ, the Eternal Priest, they will fight courageously against everything which can injure the unity of the Church, its integrity and its glory. By the purity of their doctrine and their inviolable attachment to the Chair of St. Peter, by the regularity of their lives and the force of their virtue, the members of this Union will endeavor to be in truth "the light of the world and the salt of the earth." (*Matt.* 5:13–14). They will have but one heart and one soul among them, according to the words of Our Lord to His heavenly Father: "That they be one as We also are One" (*John* 17:22); and they will carefully guard the unity of faith in the bond of fraternal charity.

III. ORGANIZATION OF THE UNION. This Priests' Universal Union has commenced humbly; if, encouraged and blessed by the Holy See, it spreads, and according to its end becomes world-wide, it would be proper that its headquarters should be in Rome, in order to radiate the influence from there over the whole Catholic world.

As the Priests' Universal Union is to be world-wide, as it has to be adapted and conformed to all minds and to all places, it must be very simple and very broad in its organization. In each diocese the members of the Priests' Universal Union will meet twice each year, if possible, under the presidency of their bishop. At the first meeting of the year, they will elect, according to their number, four or five, or a larger number of their brethren, who during the year will be charged with helping, visiting, and assisting in their spiritual and temporal needs those of their brethren who have recourse to them. At their meetings they will discuss everything which concerns the spirit of the Union. The Secretary will make a report of all the questions of interest which have been raised at the meeting.

IV. CONDITIONS OF ADMISSION. Priests who desire to become members of the Priests' Universal Union must address their petition to the diocesan Director, sending their surname and Christian name and address, and mentioning whether they are already members of a union for priests, and if so, which one. They must not have incurred any censure for doctrine, and must be of sound morals and edifying life. They must be resolved to be faithful, as far as possible, to the practices of the Union.

V. OBLIGATIONS. The priests of the Priests' Universal Union undertake: *(a)* to make on the day of their entry into it, the total consecration of themselves to Infinite Love, in union with their brethren, according to the formula in use; they will renew this consecration on the First Friday of each month and are recommended to say the "Act of Consecration and Donation" each day at the end of their thanksgiving after Mass; *(b)* to diffuse, each in his sphere of action, the knowledge of Jesus Christ, God and Man, living in the Blessed Eucharist, and of His Sacred Heart overflowing with love and mercy for souls; (c) to attend at least one of the conferences of the year, unless prevented by a serious cause; *(d)* to celebrate Holy Mass once a year for the deceased confreres, and to give an intention each day in the Holy Sacrifice of the sanctification of the clergy and the extension of the reign of Jesus Christ; *(e)* to make each evening an examination of the day from the viewpoint of conformity of the life of the priest with that of Our Lord Jesus Christ (for this examination they can use the formula given below); to make each day, preferably in the morning, a meditation, or a reading meditated on from the same point of view. For this meditation, they are recommended to make use of *The Sacred Heart and the Priesthood.*

N.B.—The employment of the morning in the ministry of hearing Confessions, or in visiting the sick, dispenses from this meditation, as does also adoration of the Blessed Sacrament, or any other form of prayer already imposed by another Sacerdotal organization.

REMARK: Although the Priests' Universal Union is specially intended for secular priests, priests of Religious Orders or Congregations can become members individually on the same conditions of admission.

Act of Consecration and Donation to Infinite Love

O INFINITE LOVE, eternal God, Principle of life, Source of being, I adore Thee in Thy sovereign Unity and the Trinity of Thy Persons.

I adore Thee in the Father, omnipotent Creator Who has made all things. I adore Thee in the Son, eternal Wisdom, by Whom all things have been made, the Word of the Father, incarnate in time in the womb of the Virgin Mary,

Jesus Christ, Redeemer and King. I adore Thee in the Holy Ghost, substantial love of the Father and the Son, in Whom are light, strength and fruitfulness.

I adore Thee, Infinite Love, hidden in the mysteries of our Faith, shedding Thy beneficent rays in the Blessed Eucharist, overflowing on Calvary and giving life to the Holy Church by the channels of the Sacraments; I adore Thee throbbing in the Heart of Jesus, Thy ineffable tabernacle, and I consecrate myself to Thee.

I give myself to Thee without fear with the fullness of my will; take possession of my being, penetrate it entirely. I am but a nothing, powerless to serve Thee, it is true, but it is Thou, Infinite Love, Who hast given life to this nothing and Who dost draw it to Thee.

Behold me, then, O Jesus, come to do Thy work of love: to labor to the utmost of my capacity, in bringing to Thy priests and through them to the entire world, the knowledge of Thy Infinite mercies, and of the sublime and tender love of Thy Heart.

I wish to accomplish Thy Will, whatever it may cost me; even to the shedding of my blood, if my blood be not unworthy to flow for Thy glory.

O Mary, Immaculate Virgin, whom Infinite Love has rendered fruitful, it is by thy virginal hands that I give and consecrate myself. Obtain for me the grace to be humble and faithful, and to devote myself without reserve to the interests of Jesus Christ, Thy adorable Son, and to the glory of His Sacred Heart.

Pope Pius XI has granted an indulgence of 300 days toties quoties for the recitation of this prayer, and a plenary indulgence once a month to all members of the Priests' Universal Union who recite it daily for a month.

Examinations to be Made Each Day

THE Heart of Jesus, the divine Priest, was dominated by three sentiments all the days of His life: an ardent thirst for the glory of His Father, a passionate desire for the salvation of the souls of His brethren, an irresistible and constant need of self-sacrifice and immolation.

Have these three sentiments dominated my heart today? What have I done today to glorify my heavenly Father? What have I undertaken for the good of my brethren? What sacrifice have I made in union with Jesus immolated?

I. Jesus, the divine Priest, willingly accepted opprobrium and humiliations to repair the glory of God. Have I today, humbled myself before God, recognizing my nothingness and my miseries, and referring to Him the glory of the good which I have accomplished by His grace? Have I received with joy the contempt and the outrages of men?

II. Jesus, the divine Priest, never thought of Himself; He left all things, stripping Himself of everything and becoming poor, in order to give Himself completely to the salvation of His brethren. What have I done today for my brethren, with my time, with my heart, with my goods; if I have not given of my material goods, have I at least used my intellectual and spiritual gifts for them?

III. Jesus, the divine Priest, having lived in a spirit of continual sacrifice, at the end offered Himself on the Cross, immolating His own life by love. Have I manifested the spirit of sacrifice in my actions this day? What sacrifice have I made today of my satisfactions of heart, of my contentment of mind, of my strength, of my repose, of my life, for the love of Jesus, and for souls?

Profound and sorrowful regrets for the shortcomings of this day. Offering to the Heart of Jesus of the good accomplished.

A Form of Consecrating Priests to the Most Sacred Heart of Jesus

*L*ORD JESUS, Who art our most loving Redeemer and a Priest forever, look mercifully on us, Thy humble suppliants, whom Thou hast been pleased to call Thy friends and partakers of Thy Priesthood. We are Thine; we wish to be Thine forever; therefore to Thy most Sacred Heart Which Thou hast shown to oppressed humanity as their only safe refuge, we dedicate and devote ourselves wholly this day. Thou Who hast promised plenteous fruit in the divine ministry to those priests who are devoted to the Sacred Heart,

make us, we beseech Thee, fit workmen in the vineyard, truly meek and humble, filled with the spirit of devotion and patience, so fired with love of Thee
that we shall never cease to enkindle and quicken the same fire of love in the
hearts of the faithful. Renew our hearts, therefore, in the fire of Thy Heart,
so that henceforth we shall desire nothing save to promote Thy glory and win
for Thee the souls whom Thou didst redeem by Thy precious Blood. Show
Thy mercy, good Shepherd, chiefly to those priests, our brethren, if there be
any such who, walking in the vanity of sense, have saddened Thee and Thy
beloved Spouse, holy Church, by their lamentable falling away from Thee.
Grant us grace to bring them back to Thine embrace, or, at least, to atone for
their crimes, to repair the harm they have done, and to lessen the sorrow they
have caused Thee, by the consolation of our love. Allow each one of us, finally,
to pray to Thee in the words of St. Augustine:

"O sweet Jesus, live Thou in me, and let the living coal of Thy love burn
brightly in my spirit, and grow into a perfect conflagration; let it burn perpetually on the altar of my heart, let it glow in my marrow, let it blaze up in the
most secret places of my soul; in the day of my consummation let me be found
totally consumed thereby in Thy presence, Who with the Father and the Holy
Ghost livest and reignest one God for ever and ever. Amen."[10]

Indulgences: *Three years for each recitation;*
           Seven years on the day of monthly retreat.

The Works by and about
Mother Louise Margaret Claret de la Touche

The Sacred Heart and the Priesthood
The Book of Infinite Love
The Little Book of the Work of Infinite Love
The Love and Service of God—Infinite Love
The Life and Work of Mother Louise Margaret Claret de la Touche
   (Containing a Message from Our Lord for the Clergy of the World)

With the printing of this volume, the first three books concerning
Mother Louise Margaret indicated above have been returned to print.
If the reader has derived benefit from this book and would like to assist
in the reprinting of the last two books, that is, *The Love and Service of*

10. This translation is taken from the *Raccolta*.

God and *The Life and Work of Mother Louise Margaret,* he should send his contributions to

Father Vergil Heier, C.M.M.
Mariannhill Missionaries
23715 Ann Arbor Trail
Dearborn Heights MI 48127

Father Heier is the official promoter in the United States of the Priests' Universal Union of the Friends of the Sacred Heart. He will be happy to send further information about this Union and the work of reprinting the books of Mother Louise Margaret to those requesting it. When sufficient funds have been obtained to reprint these last two books, they shall be republished in popular format.

SAINT BENEDICT + PRESS

Saint Benedict Press, founded in 2006, is the parent company for a variety of imprints including TAN Books, Catholic Courses, Benedict Bibles, Benedict Books, and Labora Books. The company's name pays homage to the guiding influence of the Rule of Saint Benedict and the Benedictine monks of Belmont Abbey, North Carolina, just a short distance from the company's headquarters in Charlotte, NC.

Saint Benedict Press is now a multi-media company. Its mission is to publish and distribute products reflective of the Catholic intellectual tradition and to present these products in an attractive and accessible manner.

TAN · BOOKS

TAN Books was founded in 1967, in response to the rapid decline of faith and morals in society and the Church. Since its founding, TAN Books has been committed to the preservation and promotion of the spiritual, theological and liturgical traditions of the Catholic Church. In 2008, TAN Books was acquired by Saint Benedict Press. Since then, TAN has experienced positive growth and diversification while fulfilling its mission to a new generation of readers.

TAN Books publishes over 500 titles on Thomistic theology, traditional devotions, Church doctrine, history, lives of the saints, educational resources, and booklets.

For a free catalog from Saint Benedict Press
or TAN Books, visit us online at
saintbenedictpress.com • tanbooks.com
or call us toll-free at
(800) 437-5876